About This Book

This book is written for every person who has been concerned about what is going to happen between the year 2000 A.D. and the final coming of Jesus Christ. It will also help the reader prepare for this event by providing answers from the Book of Revelation, Joseph Smith–Matthew and The Doctrine and Covenants to the following questions:

- What is the mysterious knowledge given to us by the seven churches of Asia that will help us overcome Satan and his minions during the last days?

- What is the real significance of the riders on the white and red horses?

- What is the actual role of the *144,000* servants of God?

- What trumpets have already sounded, and where do we stand in our relationship to the *Book of Revelation* time line?

- How long must Judah wait before a temple can be built in Jerusalem?

- When will the main body of the *Lost Ten Tribes of Israel* make their appearance?

- What role will the two prophets play in presenting the gospel of Jesus Christ to the Jews?

- How will the abomination of desolation take place?

- What event will take place to indicate that the missionary effort to the Gentiles is finished; and how will this calamity work as a

(continued on next page)

catalyst to motivate a remnant of Judah to accept the gospel of Jesus Christ?

- What is the role of Satan, the beast, the false prophet, and what do the numbers *666* represent?

- What sequence of events will occur just prior to the resurrection of the elect, and what will happen to the Saints who are left behind?

- How will the main harvest begin, and what will happen to those individuals who take on the mark of the beast?

- What is the meaning of the term, MYSTERY AND MOTHER OF HARLOTS, and what great city represents Babylon the Great?

- What is the sequence of events leading to Armageddon, and how will the destruction of Babylon take place?

- How will the Second Coming occur, and what rewards have been promised to the Saints who remain steadfast in obeying the commandments of God?

About the Author

The author's previous works include *Lord, Why Me?*; *But Why Do Good People Suffer?*; *Armageddon: the Warning and the Promise*; *Understanding the Gift of Mortal Life*; *How to Accept the Gift of Eternal Life*; and *The Revelation of St. John the Divine Unfolded.*

RECONCILING
the
BOOK of REVELATION
with
MORMON PROPHECIES

*A Guide to Overcoming
the Hour of Temptation
That Shall Come Upon
All the World*

(See Revelation 3:10)

——————— By ———————

Larry Moench Davis

RECONCILING
the
BOOK of REVELATION
with
MORMON PROPHECIES

Legends Library

New York

To see the complete Legends Library, visit www.legendslibrary.org

For info write to: info@digitalegend.com or call toll free: 877-222-1960

ISBN: 978-1-937735-53-1

Printed in the United States of America First Printing: August 2013

Cover design by Alisha Bishop

RECONCILING
the
BOOK of REVELATION
with
MORMON PROPHECIES

Larry Moench Davis

New York

Contents

Contents *(continued)*

Part II Reconciling *Revelation* with Mormon Prophecies

Introduction

Reconciling the book of Revelation with Mormon prophecies will require two components. Part I reviews the entire book of Revelation for content and meaning. Part II compares key Mormon prophecies with similar passages from *Revelation* to illustrate their unity and resolve.

This book reproduces the entire text of the Book of Revelation as it was written using the King James Version of the Holy Bible. To facilitate ease of comprehension, a question and answer format was used with the corresponding scripture printed immediately following the topic.

Part I

Reviewing the Book of Revelation

1

The Vision Opens

Upon entering the 21st century the world is asking the question, what shall happen in the coming years? Of all the prophets that God has placed on this earth, only one has been honored by God to see and report concerning what shall happen between 2000 A.D. and the final coming of Jesus Christ. This prophet was called John. His report was written in a book titled, *"The Revelation of St. John the Divine,"* which is located in the Holy Bible.

This revelation was given to provide a general outline concerning what shall happen and serves as a warning to all those who shall not follow God's commandment to repent. It also reminds us of the great blessings that God has promised to all who shall do His will.

Where did the material in the Book of Revelation come from?

It comes from Jesus Christ, who showed himself to John, and is given to John by an angel of the Lord who certifies that the information is accurate.

> *1 The Revelation of Jesus Christ, which God gave unto him, to shew unto his servants things which must shortly come to pass; and he sent and signified it by his angel unto his servant John:*
> *2 Who bare record of the word of God, and of the testimony of Jesus Christ, and of all things that he saw.[1]*

Since this book was written approximately 1900 years ago, is the information in this book applicable to us?

Most of the prophecies outlined in this book shall take place between 2000 A.D. and the final coming of Jesus Christ. The promise is also given that all who read and obey the words of Revelation shall be blessed.

> *3 Blessed is he that readeth, and they that hear the words of this prophecy, and keep those things which are written therein: for the time is at hand.[2]*

Where was John told to send this information?

John originally addresses this information to the seven branches of the Church of Jesus Christ in Asia. However, the term *seven*, is used as a representative term to denote all churches that belong to Jesus Christ. John tells the seven churches, that this information comes directly from Jesus Christ, who died on the cross, was taken up into heaven, and shall return at some future time.

---

1. Rev. 1:1-2
2. Rev. 1:3

4 John to the seven churches which are in Asia: Grace be unto you, and peace, from him which is, and which was, and which is to come; and from the seven Spirits which are before his throne;

5 And from Jesus Christ, who is the faithful witness, and the first begotten of the dead, and the prince of the kings of the earth. Unto him that loved us, and washed us from our sins in his own blood,

6 And hath made us kings and priests unto God and his Father; to him be glory and dominion for ever and ever. Amen.

7 Behold, he cometh with clouds; and every eye shall see him, and they also which pierced him: and all kindreds of the earth shall wail because of him. Even so, Amen.

8 I am Alpha and Omega, the beginning and the ending, saith the Lord, which is, and which was, and which is to come, the Almighty.[3]

How did John receive this revelation?

After he is banished to the Isle of Patmos, John receives this information from the Lord and is told to write what he sees and send it to the seven churches in Asia.

9 I John, who also am your brother, and companion in tribulation, and in the kingdom and patience of Jesus Christ, was in the isle that is called Patmos, for the word of God, and for the testimony of Jesus Christ.

10 I was in the Spirit on the Lord's day, and heard behind me a great voice, as of a trumpet,

11 Saying, I am Alpha and Omega, the first and the last: and, What thou seest, write in a book, and send it unto the seven churches which are in Asia; unto Ephesus, and unto Smyrna, and unto Pergamos, and unto Thyatira, and unto Sardis, and unto Philadelphia, and unto Laodicea.[4]

---

3. Rev. 1:4-8
4. Rev. 1:9-11

What did John see in the initial scene?

He witnesses a heavenly vision in which he sees Jesus Christ in His glorified, resurrected state.

> *12 And I turned to see the voice that spake with me. And being turned, I saw seven golden candlesticks;*
> *13 And in the midst of the seven candlesticks one like unto the Son of man, clothed with a garment down to the foot, and girt about the paps with a golden girdle.*
> *14 His head and his hairs were white like wool, as white as snow; and his eyes were as a flame of fire;*
> *15 And his feet like unto fine brass, as if they burned in a furnace; and his voice as the sound of many waters.*
> *16 And he had in his right hand seven stars: and out of his mouth went a sharp twoedged sword: and his countenance was as the sun shineth in his strength.*
> *17 And when I saw him, I fell at his feet as dead. And he laid his right hand upon me, saying unto me, Fear not; I am the first and the last:*
> *18 I am he that liveth, and was dead; and, behold, I am alive for evermore, Amen; and have the keys of hell and of death.[5]*

John was commissioned to write about three different topics, what were they?

He is told to write about the things he sees that pertain to his current day and of the things that shall be shown to him concerning past and future events.

> *19 Write the things which thou hast seen, and the things which are, and the things which shall be hereafter;[6]*

---

5. Rev. 1: 12-18
6. Rev. 1: 19

What are the seven stars and the seven golden candlesticks that John saw?

The seven stars are the spiritual leaders of the seven churches and the seven golden candlesticks represent the seven churches in Asia. *Again*, the seven leaders and the seven churches are used to represent all leaders and all churches that belong to Jesus Christ.

> *20 The mystery of the seven stars which thou sawest in my right hand, and the seven golden candlesticks. The seven stars are the angels of the seven churches: and the seven candlesticks which thou sawest are the seven churches.*[7]

---

7. Rev. 1: 20

2

Ephesus, Smyrna, Pergamos, & Thyatira

As the angel begins to unfold the mysteries of heaven, John prepares to write to the seven churches in Asia.

What information did Jesus Christ want John to impart to the church in Ephesus?

He is to inform the leader of this church that the information sent is from Jesus Christ. The Lord is aware of their good works, but the Savior is concerned that they are losing their love and faith in Him by not exercising the constant need to repent. He commends them for disapproving the actions of the Nicolaitans. This cult believes that sexual immortality is not sinful because it only involves the physical body and not the soul. Their goal is to seduce the disciples of Christ into participating in pagan feasts and rituals involving sexual acts. The Lord then gives hope by mentioning the blessings that await those who remain righteous to the end.

> *1 Unto the angel of the church of Ephesus write; These things saith he that holdeth the seven stars in his right hand, who walketh in the midst of the seven golden candlesticks;*
>
> *2 I know thy works, and thy labour, and thy patience, and how thou canst not bear them which are evil: and thou hast tried them which say they are apostles, and are not, and hast found them liars:*
>
> *3 And hast borne, and hast patience, and for my name's sake hast laboured, and hast not fainted.*
>
> *4 Nevertheless I have somewhat against thee, because thou hast left thy first love.*
>
> *5 Remember therefore from whence thou art fallen, and repent, and do the first works; or else I will come unto thee quickly, and will remove thy candlestick out of his place, except thou repent.*
>
> *6 But this thou hast, that thou hatest the deeds of the Nicolaitans, which I also hate.*
>
> *7 He that hath an ear, let him hear what the Spirit saith unto the churches; To him that overcometh will I give to eat of the tree of life, which is in the midst of the paradise of God.[1]*

To the church in Smyrna, what information were they suppose to receive?

John is to communicate to the leader of this branch of the Church that the Savior is the author behind the letter. The Lord is aware of their good works, and wants them to know that, even though many were experiencing poverty, they are rich because they shall become joint heirs with Him if they remain faithful. The Lord acknowledges the existence of some in the area who

---

1. Rev.2:1-7

say they are Jews, but who follow the works of Satan. He then gives hope by mentioning the blessings that await those who overcome, even though it may require a martyr's death.

> *8 And unto the angel of the church in Smyrna write; These things saith the first and the last, which was dead, and is alive;*
>
> *9 I know thy works, and tribulation, and poverty, (but thou art rich) and I know the blasphemy of them which say they are Jews, and are not, but are the synagogue of Satan.*
>
> *10 Fear none of those things which thou shalt suffer: behold, the devil shall cast some of you into prison, that ye may be tried; and ye shall have tribulation ten days: be thou faithful unto death, and I will give thee a crown of life.*
>
> *11 He that hath an ear, let him hear what the Spirit saith unto the churches; He that overcometh shall not be hurt of the second death.*[2]

What words of advice was John asked to send to the church in Pergamos?

He is tasked to write to the leader of this church and say that the Lord is aware of their good works and is pleased that they have not denied the faith, even though it has cost one disciple his life. However, He is concerned because there are some in their congregation who follow the doctrine of Balaam by compromising their values (in order to fit in with the norms of society) by participating in fornication and the eating of food that has been used in forbidden cult rituals. The Savior is also displeased that some are participating in Nicolaitans rituals and warns of their need to repent or suffer the consequences. Hope is then given concerning the blessings that await the righteous who endure to the end.

---

2. Rev. 2: 8-11

12 And to the angel of the church in Pergamos write; These things saith he which hath the sharp sword with two edges; 13 I know thy works, and where thou dwellest, even where Satan's seat is: and thou holdest fast my name, and hast not denied my faith, even in those days wherein Antipas was my faithful martyr, who was slain among you, where Satan dwelleth.

14 But I have a few things against thee, because thou hast there them that hold the doctrine of Balaam, who taught Balac to cast a stumblingblock before the children of Israel, to eat things sacrificed unto idols, and to commit fornication.

15 So hast thou also them that hold the doctrine of the Nicolaitans, which thing I hate.

16 Repent; or else I will come unto thee quickly, and will fight against them with the sword of my mouth.

17 He that hath an ear, let him hear what the Spirit saith unto the churches; To him that overcometh will I give to eat of the hidden manna, and will give him a white stone, and in the stone a new name written, which no man knoweth saving he that receiveth it.[3]

To the church in Thyatira, what important message were they to receive?

John is to explain to their leader that the words in his letter come from the Son of God. The Lord knows their works of charity and service. However, He is troubled because there is a woman (a self-proclaimed prophet) in their congregation who is seducing some members through fornication and the eating of unclean food. The Lord wants the entire congregation to know that whoever commits fornication with her shall be under condemnation unless they repent and that He shall give each according to his works. He commends those who are holding fast and confirms the existence of more rewards for those who

---

3. Rev. 2:12-17

overcome and keep the Lord's commandments unto the end.

> *18 And unto the angel of the church in Thyatira write;
> These things saith the Son of God, who hath his eyes like
> unto a flame of fire, and his feet are like fine brass;*
> *19 I know thy works, and charity, and service, and faith,
> and thy patience, and thy works; and the last to be more
> than the first.*
> *20 Notwithstanding I have a few things against thee,
> because thou sufferest that woman Jezebel, which calleth
> herself a prophetess, to teach and to seduce my servants to
> commit fornication, and to eat things sacrificed unto idols.*
> *21 And I gave her space to repent of her fornication; and
> she repented not.*
> *22 Behold, I will cast her into a bed, and them that commit
> adultery with her into great tribulation, except they repent
> of their deeds.*
> *23 And I will kill her children with death; and all the
> churches shall know that I am he which searcheth the
> reins and hearts: and I will give unto every one of you
> according to your works.*
> *24 But unto you I say, and unto the rest in Thyatira, as
> many as have not this doctrine, and which have not known
> the depths of Satan, as they speak; I will put upon you
> none other burden.*
> *25 But that which ye have already hold fast till I come.*
> *26 And he that overcometh, and keepeth my works unto
> the end, to him will I give power over the nations:*
> *27 And he shall rule them with a rod of iron; as the
> vessels of a potter shall they be broken to shivers: even
> as I received of my Father.*
> *28 And I will give him the morning star.*
> *29 He that hath an ear, let him hear what the Spirit saith
> unto the churches.[4]*

---

4. Rev. 2:18-29

3

Sardis, Philadelphia, & Laodiceans

John, after being shown the information that the Lord wants sent to the churches in Ephesus, Smyrna, Pergamos, and Thyatira, is ready to receive the words for the churches in Sardis, Philadelphia, and Laodicea.

Concerning the church in Sardis, what information did Jesus Christ want their leader to receive?

He wants this leader to know that He (Jesus Christ) is the individual who caused this letter to be written, and that He knows that some members are near death (with respect to activity in His gospel). Thus, their works are not perfect in His eyes. To improve, they need to repent and strengthen the testimonies of others who are near spiritual death. They are also cautioned to be vigilant and hold fast so they can be ready when their time is finished. The Lord commends the few who are holding steady and then outlines more blessings available for those who attain the Kingdom of God.

> *1 And unto the angel of the church in Sardis write; These things saith he that hath the seven Spirits of God, and the seven stars; I know thy works, that thou hast a name that thou livest, and art dead.*
>
> *2 Be watchful, and strengthen the things which remain, that are ready to die: for I have not found thy works perfect before God.*
>
> *3 Remember therefore how thou hast received and heard, and hold fast, and repent. If therefore thou shalt not watch, I will come on thee as a thief, and thou shalt not know what hour I will come upon thee.*
>
> *4 Thou hast a few names even in Sardis which have not defiled their garments; and they shall walk with me in white: for they are worthy.*
>
> *5 He that overcometh, the same shall be clothed in white raiment; and I will not blot out his name out of the book of life, but I will confess his name before my Father, and before his angels.*
>
> *6 He that hath an ear, let him hear what the Spirit saith unto the churches.*[1]

What information did Jesus Christ want sent to the leader of the church in Philadelphia?

John is to affirm that the information in the letter comes from the Savior. He knows their works and commends the members of the church for keeping His word and not denying His name. He again condemns those who say they are Jews but do not live by Jewish principles. To those who keep His word (commandments)[2] the Lord said He shall protect them from the hour of temptation that shall come upon the entire world. The

---

1. Rev. 3:1-6
2. Rev. 14:12

Lord then mentions several more rewards that shall be given to those who overcome.

> *7 And to the angel of the church in Philadelphia write; These things saith he that is holy, he that is true, he that hath the key of David, he that openeth, and no man shutteth; and shutteth, and no man openeth;*
>
> *8 I know thy works: behold, I have set before thee an open door, and no man can shut it: for thou hast a little strength, and hast kept my word, and hast not denied my name.*
>
> *9 Behold, I will make them of the synagogue of Satan, which say they are Jews, and are not, but do lie; behold, I will make them to come and worship before thy feet, and to know that I have loved thee.*
>
> *10 Because thou hast kept the word of my patience, I also will keep thee from the hour of temptation, which shall come upon all the world, to try them that dwell upon the earth.*
>
> *11 Behold, I come quickly: hold that fast which thou hast, that no man take thy crown.*
>
> *12 Him that overcometh will I make a pillar in the temple of my God, and he shall go no more out: and I will write upon him the name of my God, and the name of the city of my God, which is new Jerusalem, which cometh down out of heaven from my God: and I will write upon him my new name.*
>
> *13 He that hath an ear, let him hear what the Spirit saith unto the churches.[3]*

Pertaining to the church in Laodicea, what words of advice were they to receive?

They are to know that Jesus Christ is the author of this letter. That the Savior is aware the members are only lukewarm

---

3. Rev. 3:7-13

in following His commandments. This is because they are too rich and comfortable, whereas in reality, they are miserable, poor, and blind in things pertaining to the saving principles of the gospel. They are to know that Christ rebukes those He loves and if they would repent, He will return to them. Again, more blessings are outlined for those who endure to the end.

> *14 And unto the angel of the church of the Laodiceans write; These things saith the Amen, the faithful and true witness, the beginning of the creation of God;*
>
> *15 I know thy works, that thou art neither cold nor hot: I would thou wert cold or hot.*
>
> *16 So then because thou art lukewarm, and neither cold nor hot, I will spue thee out of my mouth.*
>
> *17 Because thou sayest, I am rich, and increased with goods, and have need of nothing; and knowest not that thou art wretched, and miserable, and poor, and blind, and naked:*
>
> *18 I counsel thee to buy of me gold tried in the fire, that thou mayest be rich; and white raiment, that thou mayest be clothed, and that the shame of thy nakedness do not appear; and anoint thine eyes with eyesalve, that thou mayest see.*
>
> *19 As many as I love, I rebuke and chasten: be zealous therefore, and repent.*
>
> *20 Behold, I stand at the door, and knock: if any man hear my voice, and open the door, I will come in to him, and will sup with him, and he with me.*
>
> *21 To him that overcometh will I grant to sit with me in my throne, even as I also overcame, and am set down with my Father in his throne.*
>
> *22 He that hath an ear, let him hear what the Spirit saith unto the churches.[4]*

---

4. Rev. 3:14-22

How does the information pertaining to the seven churches help one prepare for the approaching challenges concerning the end of time events?

As many have discovered, the Book of Revelation is similar to an onion, as the surface is uncovered a more meaningful precept appears. An excellent example of this is found in the information that Christ wanted sent to His seven churches in Asia Minor. It should also be noted that these seven churches were selected for a very specific reason, this is because each church was experiencing a particular challenge that pertained directly to what the followers of Christ would encounter during the time leading to the Second Coming. Thus an understanding of these precise events shall help the Saints prepare for the tribulations that shall soon occur.

For example, the letter sent to His church in Ephesus contained the words: *"I know thy works, and thy labour, and thy patience, and how thou canst not bear them which are evil: and thou hast tried them which say they are apostles, and are not, and hast found them liars."*[5] In this letter the Saints are warned that (in the last days) the real danger to the followers of Christ shall not come from outside His church, but from within; in other words, as Christ was betrayed by Judas, the Saints shall be betrayed by members from their own congregations. Thus they need to take action to protect themselves against those who pretend to be virtuous, but who in actuality, are wolves in sheep clothing.

Now observe this warning sent to His church in Smyrna: *"Fear none of those things which thou shalt suffer: behold, the devil shall cast some of you into prison, that ye may be tried; and ye shall have tribulation ten days: be thou faithful unto death, and I will give thee a crown of life."*[6] As the time of

5. Rev. 2:2
6. Rev. 2:10

the end approaches, lawlessness, mayhem, and rebellion shall abound. The Saints will be targeted because of the threat they pose to the kingdom of Satan. Some shall be cast into prison; others will suffer even unto death. However, this tribulation shall be limited in scope, and those who endure to the end shall be rewarded with eternal life.

These words of advice were sent to the church in Pergamos: *"But I have a few things against thee, because thou hast there them that hold the doctrine of Balaam, who taught Balac to cast a stumbling block before the children of Israel, to eat things sacrificed unto idols, and to commit fornication, So hast thou also them that hold the doctrine of the Nicolaitans, which thing I hate."*[7]

These words of warning explain how the traitors within the Church shall *specifically* betray their fellow members prior to the Second Coming. Some shall use the doctrine of Balaam by covertly giving the followers of Satan the information they need concerning how best to attack and destroy the children of God. While others shall have great success by convincing many that evil is good and good is evil.

To His church in Thyatira the Savior counseled: *"Notwithstanding I have a few things against thee, because thou sufferest that woman Jezebel, which calleth herself a prophetess, to teach and to seduce my servants to commit fornication, and to eat things sacrificed unto idols. . . . Behold I will cast her into a bed, and them that commit adultery with her into great tribulation, except they repent of their deeds. And I will kill her children with death; and all the churches shall know that I am he which searcheth the reins and hearts; and I will give unto every one of you according to your works."*[8] From the scriptures we learn that the name Jezebel stems from a person who was born around 890 B.C. She was the daughter of Ethbaal, the king of Zidon. She married Ahab, the king of

---

7. Rev. 2:14
8. Rev. 2:20-23

Israel, and was responsible for encouraging Ahab to forsake the commandments of God by introducing the worship of Baal into northern Israel.[9] To assist this endeavor she employed 450 prophets of Baal and 400 prophets of the groves to sway the children of Israel into worshiping false idols and participating in immoral behavior. Additionally, she was the driving force behind the murder of many of the Lord's prophets.[10] She also possessed a subtle ability to solve a problem with complete disregard for human decency. An example of this occurred when King Ahab tried to appropriate a neighbor's land for his own pleasure. During the course of this action Ahab's efforts were rebuffed leaving him greatly disheartened. Upon learning of his dilemma, Jezebel devised a plan to lure the landowner into a plot where the unsuspecting property-owner was killed, thereby allowing Ahab to obtain his prize.[11] In short, Jezebel was the epitome of wickedness. She was so successful in causing Ahab to do evil in the sight of the Lord, that it was said, that he (Ahab) did more to provoke the Lord than all the kings of Israel who lived before him.[12]

But who was the Jezebel of Revelation? Just the fact that the Savior referred to her as *"that woman Jezebel"* indicates that she harbored many of the same characteristics of the original Jezebel, with one added distinction. This Jezebel claimed to be a prophetess.

Thus this warning to His church in Thyatira informs the end time Saints that a third Jezebel shall arise during the last days, and that this woman will possess many of the same traits already exhibited by the first two Jezebels. More information will be provided concerning this woman in chapter 13.

In the letter to His church in Sardis we find these words of caution: *"Be watchful, and strengthen the things which remain, that are ready to die: for I have not found thy works perfect*

---

9. 1 Kings 16:31; 18:18   12. 1 Kings 16:13
10. 1 Kings 18:19; 19:10
11. 1 Kings 21:8-15

before God."[13] The words *"be watchful"* carry a very special meaning. This expression conveys the notion that we need to be alert (for something is about to happen). In the meantime, we are to remain steadfast and strengthen those around us whose faith is slowly ebbing away.

But what is about to happen? To learn more, we must examine these comforting words that were sent to His church in Philadelphia: *"Because thou hast kept the word of my patience, I also will keep thee from the hour of temptation, which shall come upon all the world, to try them that dwell upon the earth."*[14] From this passage we discover that those who have patiently kept the commandments of God shall, *as a reward*, be kept from having to suffer the trials and tribulations that shall come upon the entire earth. This will occur as the elect Saints of God are resurrected from harm's way just before the Lord allows the beast and false prophet to separate the righteous from the wicked. (Details concerning how this shall occur will be discussed in Chapter 14.)

For those who are left behind, what should they do? The answer to this question is found in the words of counsel given to His church in Laodicea, *"I know thy works, that thou art neither cold nor hot: I would thou wert cold or hot. So then because thou art lukewarm, and neither cold nor hot, I will spue thee out of my mouth. Because thou sayest, I am rich, and increased with goods, and have need of nothing; and knowest not that art wretched, and miserable, and poor, and blind, and naked: I counsel thee to buy of me gold tried in the fire, that thou mayest be rich; and white raiment, that thou mayest be clothed, and that the shame of thy nakedness do not appear; and anoint thine eyes with eyesalve, that thou mayest see."*[15] The important point to glean from this information is that the time for sitting on the fence has come to an end; those who have failed to totally commit to keeping the commandments of Jesus Christ (because it

---

13. Rev. 3:2
14. Rev. 3:10
15. Rev. 3:15-18

would hamper their lifestyle) must now choose sides. However, all must understand that to choose the Lord will not be easy, for we are told that those who follow this course shall be tried as gold in the fire, but if they remain faithful to the end, they shall have the opportunity to be clothed in the white raiment that symbolizes eternal life. In contrast, those who choose to maintain the comfort of their current surroundings shall eventually be cast into hell where they will experience the second death for at least a thousand years. To help make this decision one should consider the words Elijah posed to the followers of the first Jezebel: *"How long halt ye between two opinions? If the Lord be God, follow him: but if Baal, then follow him."*[16] In other words, *how long is it prudent to wait before one decides whom to follow? If the Lord is God, follow Him, however, if Satan is God then choose him.* Thus the decision is up to us, the Lord just wants all to know that he is standing nearby and ready to help: *"Behold, I stand at the door, and knock: if any man hear my voice, and open the door, I will come in to him, and will sup with him, and he with me."*[17]

What is the most important information we need to glean from the writings of John to the seven churches in Asia?

Since these seven churches represent all churches of Jesus Christ, the problems experienced in each church represent the problems encountered in all His churches. This is why it is important to review these concerns. A summary of these offenses committed by the members of these seven churches are listed below:

- They display a lack of faith and are not willing to repent.[18]

---

16. 1 Kings 18:21   18. Rev. 2:21
17. Rev. 3:20

- They are willing to be led into fornication, adultery, and other immoral conduct by the seducing servants of Satan.[19]
- They are unwilling to strengthen their fellowmen who stray from the teachings of Jesus Christ.[20]
- They are not willing to hold fast and endure to the end.[21]
- They are lukewarm in obeying the commandments of Jesus Christ.[22]
- They are unwilling to accept rebuke and chastening from the Lord.[23]

---

19. Rev. 2:14   22. Rev. 3:16
20. Rev. 3:2   23. Rev. 3:19
21. Rev. 2:10

4

The Vision of God, Elders, & Beasts

After John receives the information that the Lord wants sent to the churches in Sardis, Philadelphia, and Laodicea, he is allowed to ascend into heaven to witness an incredible sight.

Immediately after his ascension, what did John behold?

As he looks, he sees God the Eternal Father sitting on His throne in all His power and glory.

> *1 After this I looked, and, behold, a door was opened in heaven: and the first voice which I heard was as it were of a trumpet talking with me; which said, Come up hither, and I will shew thee things which must be hereafter.*
> *2 And immediately I was in the spirit: and, behold, a throne was set in heaven, and one sat on the throne.*

3 And he that sat was to look upon like a jasper and a
sardine stone: and there was a rainbow round about the
throne, in sight like unto an emerald.[1]

Who did John see seated before the throne?

He observes twenty-four elders wearing gold crowns upon
their heads, dressed in white clothing. Though the twenty-four
elders are from the seven churches, they represent all elders
who have distinguished themselves by the manner in which they
have magnified their work in the ministry. He also sees seven
lamps, which represent the seven Spirits (special witnesses) of
God sent forth unto all the earth.[2]

4 And round about the throne were four and twenty seats:
and upon the seats I saw four and twenty elders sitting,
clothed in white raiment; and they had on their heads
crowns of gold.
5 And out of the throne proceeded lightnings and thunderings
and voices: and there were seven lamps of fire burning before
the throne, which are the seven Spirits of God.[3]

What else did John observe that was round about the throne?

He sees four beasts worshipping their creator. These four living creatures, the lion, the calf, the man, and the eagle—though
individual beasts—symbolize the different species that God has
created. They all worship God in response to the joy they receive
in being allowed to be part of His creations.

6 And before the throne there was a sea of glass like unto
crystal: and in the midst of the throne, and round about
the throne, were four beasts full of eyes before and behind.

1. Rev. 4:1-3
2. Rev. 5:6
3. Rev. 4:4-5

7 And the first beast was like a lion, and the second beast like a calf, and the third beast had a face as a man, and the fourth beast was like a flying eagle.

8 And the four beasts had each of them six wings about him; and they were full of eyes within: and they rest not day and night, saying, Holy, holy, holy, Lord God Almighty, which was, and is, and is to come.

9 And when those beasts give glory and honour and thanks to him that sat on the throne, who liveth for ever and ever,

10 The four and twenty elders fall down before him that sat on the throne, and worship him that liveth for ever and ever, and cast their crowns before the throne, saying,

11 Thou art worthy, O Lord, to receive glory and honour and power: for thou hast created all things, and for thy pleasure they are and were created.[4]

---

4. Rev. 4:6-11

5

Acceptance of a Book by Jesus Christ

A s John looks, he witnesses an unusual occurrence that is taking place.

What did John see that caused tears to well up within his eyes?

John is distressed to see that many of the elders are very concerned about a book being held by God and sealed with seven seals. An angel asks if there was anyone worthy to open the book. Just when it appears that no one is qualified, the Lamb (Jesus Christ) steps forward and takes the book from the hand of God the Father. A great sense of joy permeates the gathering because the Savior is qualified to open the book.

1 And I saw in the right hand of him that sat on the throne a book written within and on the backside, sealed with seven seals.

2 And I saw a strong angel proclaiming with a loud voice, Who is worthy to open the book, and to loose the seals thereof?

3 And no man in heaven, nor in earth, neither under the earth, was able to open the book, neither to look thereon.

4 And I wept much, because no man was found worthy to open and to read the book, neither to look thereon.

5 And one of the elders saith unto me, Weep not: behold, the Lion of the tribe of Juda, the Root of David, hath prevailed to open the book, and to loose the seven seals thereof.

6 And I beheld, and, lo, in the midst of the throne and of the four beasts, and in the midst of the elders, stood a Lamb as it had been slain, having seven horns and seven eyes, which are the seven Spirits of God sent forth into all the earth.

7 And he came and took the book out of the right hand of him that sat upon the throne.

8 And when he had taken the book, the four beasts and four and twenty elders fell down before the Lamb, having every one of them harps, and golden vials full of odours, which are the prayers of saints.

9 And they sung a new song, saying, Thou art worthy to take the book, and to open the seals thereof: for thou wast slain, and hast redeemed us to God by thy blood out of every kindred, and tongue, and people, and nation;

10 And hast made us unto our God kings and priests: and we shall reign on the earth.

11 And I beheld, and I heard the voice of many angels round about the throne and the beasts and the elders: and the number of them was ten thousand times ten thousand, and thousands of thousands;

12 Saying with a loud voice, Worthy is the Lamb that was slain to receive power, and riches, and wisdom, and strength, and honour, and glory, and blessing.

13 And every creature which is in heaven, and on the earth, and under the earth, and such as are in the sea, and all that are in them, heard I saying, Blessing, and honour, and glory, and power, be unto him that sitteth upon the throne, and unto the Lamb for ever and ever.

14 And the four beasts said, Amen. And the four and twenty elders fell down and worshipped him that liveth for ever and ever.[1]

---

1. Rev. 5:1-14

6

Opening First – Sixth Seals

Given that only the Savior was qualified to open this book, John must have been very curious to know what was inside. Soon his interest would be satisfied.

What was in the book that was sealed with the seven seals?

Among other things, the sealed book contains a description of a major happening during each one thousand year period since Adam and Eve. According to Archbishop Ussher's Chronology of the Bible, slightly over six thousand years have passed since Adam and Eve left the Garden of Eden (from approximately 4000 B.C. to 2012 A.D.). Therefore, the first seal outlines a major event of the first thousand years, the second seal lists a major occurrence of the second thousand years and so on until the seven-thousand-year point has been reached.

Who did John see when the first seal was opened?

He observes a person riding a white horse with a crown on his head and armed with a bow going forth to conquer.

This individual is Jesus Christ leading the charge against evil. He wears a crown because He is king over the forces of good.[1] The white horse represents a worthy mount that has the honor of carrying one who is pure and righteous. The bow (without arrows) signifies that He conquers only with the power of His word, the true and everlasting gospel. This occurs at the beginning of the first thousand period of time (4000 B.C. to 3000 B.C.).

During this thousand-year period the Savior, as Commander and Chief, was very effective in establishing His gospel among His followers throughout the land. In achieving this accomplishment, His deputy commanders, such as Adam, Seth, Jared, and Enoch, provided immense support.

> *1 And I saw when the Lamb opened one of the seals, and I heard, as it were the noise of thunder, one of the four beasts saying, Come and see.*
> *2 And I saw, and behold a white horse: and he that sat on him had a bow; and a crown was given unto him: and he went forth conquering, and to conquer.[2]*

When the second seal was opened, what did John witness?

He sees a person upon a red horse. This person is given a great sword and has power to take peace from the earth.

This person is Satan. The color red (in this case) represents evil,[3] thus he rides on a red horse and eventually shall be known as the red dragon.[4] He leads the forces of evil in his fight against Christ for the souls of men.

---

1. Rev. 14:14
2. Rev. 6:1-2

3. Gaskill, Alonzo L. *The Lost Language of Symbolism*, 100, Deseret Book SLC, Utah
4. Rev. 12:3, 9

This second thousand-year period (3000 B.C. to 2000 B.C.) began with high expectations, in that Enoch was able to establish such a righteous city that it was translated up to heaven.[5] However, storm clouds were gathering as Satan assembled his forces and began to war against the followers of Christ. Eventually, Satan was able to achieve remarkable results. He was so successful in promulgating evil that it was necessary for God to send a worldwide flood to cleanse the earth, so His future posterity could be raised in a more righteous environment.

Thus, the battle had commenced, however, only one individual shall ride forth at the end of this war wearing crowns of victory upon his head.

> *3 And when he had opened the second seal, I heard the second beast say, Come and see.*
> *4 And there went out another horse that was red: and power was given to him that sat thereon to take peace from the earth, and that they should kill one another: and there was given unto him a great sword.[6]*

What happened as the third seal was broken?

A rider on a black horse holding a pair of balances in his hand comes into view. Simultaneously, John hears a voice speaking of wheat and barley. What does this mean? After the worldwide flood, Noah and his sons were able to establish a righteous following, and *again*, the gospel of Christ was preached among Noah's posterity. However, it did not take long until Satan once again began to tempt the children of God. By the time the third thousand-year period (2000 B.C. to 1000 B.C.) had arrived, the righteous posterity of Noah had been seriously diminished.

How frustrating this must have been for the Messiah to bear, due to the fact that only about five hundred years had elapsed

---

5. Gen. 5:22-24
6. Rev. 6:3-4

since the great flood had terminated almost all earthy life. How does the Lord try to reverse a people bent on destruction from repeating another catastrophic mistake? The answer is found in the words given to John. The pair of balances represent judgment, such as, *"Thou art weighed in the balances, and art found wanting."*[7] The blackness is symbolic of great suffering and a measure of wheat and barley indicates that this suffering is caused from famine. Therefore, this is the punishment that was decreed upon the children of God in hopes that it would cause them to repent and turn to their Savior for salvation.

It is interesting to note that around 2000 B.C. Abraham's brother Haran died of starvation thereby causing Abraham to move to Canaan. Additionally, a famine forced Jacob to move his family to Egypt where Joseph could ensure they were properly fed and nurtured. This occurred about 1750 B.C. Though this punishment seems extremely harsh, the Lord did not forsake His people. He provided other prophets and kings, such as Moses, Joshua, Samuel, and David, to bless and support the house of Israel. Nevertheless, *again* Satan would not yield, he simply intensified his efforts to captivate and subjugate the souls of all mankind.

> 5 *And when he had opened the third seal, I heard the third beast say, Come and see. And I beheld, and lo a black horse; and he that sat on him had a pair of balances in his hand.*
> 6 *And I heard a voice in the midst of the four beasts say, A measure of wheat for a penny, and three measures of barley for a penny; and see thou hurt not the oil and the wine.*[8]

---

7. Daniel 5:27
8. Rev. 6:5-6

When the fourth seal was opened, what did John see?

He beholds a person (representing death) riding upon a pale horse. This person is given power over a fourth part of the earth to kill with sword, hunger, death, and wild beasts. It was during this fourth thousand-year period (1000 B.C. to 1 B.C.) that some of the greatest accomplishments and most terrible calamities befell the children of God.

At the beginning of this thousand-year period, the Lord, through Solomon, was able to construct a temple wherein the Israelites could worship their Creator and receive wonderful blessings. Nevertheless, in conjunction with this prosperity, pride and selfishness soon began to permeate the hearts of the tribes of Israel. Consequently, *again* the Lord was forced to take action to quell their descent into the arms of the adversary. Since famine had achieved only limited success, something more devastating was required to stop their slide into oblivion. As a result, the decision was made to allow the Israelites to experience a type of death and hell in hopes of encouraging penitence for their sins. The dye was cast: About 721 B.C., ten of the twelve tribes of Israel were captured by the Assyrians and, after being exiled to Assyria, eventually fled into the northern countries. Subsequently, Nebuchadnezzar invaded Jerusalem and conquered the remaining tribes. In due course, they were forced to trade their beloved Jerusalem for Babylonian captivity. While this was devastating for the house of Israel, it was only the beginning of their experience with bondage and exile. During the ensuing years, Israel would continue to feel the torment from living under the heels of Medo-Persia, Greek, and Roman rule.

7 And when he had opened the fourth seal, I heard the voice of the fourth beast say, Come and see.
8 And I looked, and behold a pale horse: and his name that sat on him was Death, and Hell followed with him. And power was given unto them over the fourth part of the earth, to kill with sword, and with hunger, and with death, and with the beasts of the earth.[9]

As the fifth seal was broken, what heart-breaking scene did John view?

He sees great numbers of Saints slain for the word of God; but what precipitated this ominous vision?

Having experienced virtually constant persecution for almost five hundred years, the Israelites were given a great opportunity. Their prophets had predicted that their Messiah (King) would personally come to earth to help them in their hour of need. However, instead of arriving as their Commander and Chief, ready to take over the reins of government and subdue their enemies, He came as a tiny babe, born of humble parents. It was His mission to set an example, and teach His Saints how to live so they could return to His presence upon completion of mortal life. To accomplish this, it was necessary for Him to perform the Atonement so the Saints could, through repentance, obtain forgiveness for their sins. However, instead of recognizing this tiny babe as their long-sought Savior, they were duped by their own blindness and by the blindness of the Jewish leaders who insisted that Christ was nothing more than a clever imposter who represented a threat to their power and control. As a result, the majority of the tribe of Judah rejected His teachings and conspired with their enemies to arrest and crucify the Savior near the hill of Golgotha. Hence, one of the greatest opportunities

---

9. Rev. 6:7-8

to regain their freedom and esteem simply evaporated before their eyes.

But, all was not lost. Christ, during His life on earth, was able to ordain twelve apostles, establish His Church, and provide a way to obtain salvation through the Atonement for all who sincerely want to gain eternal life. During this time, Satan and his followers were desperately trying to, not only kill the Lord, but also stamp out any vestiges of His work on earth. The adversary was so successful that within forty years from the death of the Messiah, the Roman general Titus had conquered Jerusalem, dispersed the Jews, and began a bloodbath that resulted in thousands of Saints (over the next several centuries) being martyred for the word of God. All of this occurred during the fifth thousand-year period of 1 B.C. to 1000 A.D.

> *9 And when he had opened the fifth seal, I saw under the altar the souls of them that were slain for the word of God, and for the testimony which they held:*
> *10 And they cried with a loud voice, saying, How long, O Lord, holy and true, dost thou not judge and avenge our blood on them that dwell on the earth?*
> *11 And white robes were given unto every one of them; and it was said unto them, that they should rest yet for a little season, until their fellowservants also and their brethren, that should be killed as they were, should be fulfilled.*[10]

What happened when the sixth seal was opened?

John observes a great earthquake, the sun turns black, the moon becomes as blood, the stars fall from the heaven, and men scurry about trying to find some protective shelter from the wrath of God.

---

10. Rev. 6:9-11

But how did mankind arrive at the point where they feared that God's wrath would soon be unleashed upon their own heads? A clue is provided by John when he recorded: *"And I saw another angel fly in the midst of heaven, having the everlasting gospel to preach unto them that dwell on the earth, and to every nation, and kindred, and tongue, and people. Saying with a loud voice, Fear God, and give glory to him; for the hour of his judgment has come:*[11]

Thus the key to understanding the main event of the sixth seal (1000 A.D. to 2000 A.D.) is to carefully examine what the angels (who have been given power over this period of time) are tasked to accomplish before this judgment occurs. When John discovers that the angel he sees holds the power to dispense the everlasting gospel to all who dwell on the face of the earth, and Matthew confirms that the *"gospel of the kingdom shall be preached in all the world for a witness unto all nations; and then shall the end come,"*[12] it becomes apparent that the major event of the sixth seal is not the judgment described in the opening of the sixth seal, but instead the missionary work that must be accomplished before that judgment can take place. To see if this conclusion is accurate let's examine the historical record.

As mankind entered the sixth thousand-period of 1000 A.D. to 2000 A.D., it is evident that Satan and his forces had severely decimated the house of Israel and the Church of Jesus Christ. All twelve tribes of Israel, because of disobedience, were either lost or scattered throughout the Gentile nations. The Church Christ established, had been eviscerated by persecution, captivity, and betrayal. Historians would eventually refer to this period of wholesale apostasy as the *dark ages*. By the mid-sixteenth century, the word of the Lord had either been compromised or erased from all scripture. However, the winds of change were in the air.

---

11. Rev. 14:6, 7
12. Matt. 24:14

It was about this time that certain disciples stepped forward and courageously, in the face of martyrdom, translated and published the biblical teachings of Christ to the world. At the turn of the nineteenth century, the Lord was able to bring to pass a marvelous work and wonder,[13] thus enabling Christianity to blossom as a rose. Additionally, in 1948, the Lord provided the necessary support that helped the nation of Israel to become a reality, thus creating a home for the return of her children.

Once again missionaries were sent to roam the earth in search of those individuals who were seeking truth and light. As a result of this divinely directed missionary effort, a vast group of converts have been gathered into the fold. This shall continue into the twenty-first Century and shall become known as the golden age of missionary work.

In due time, a special group symbolized by the *144,000* servants of God shall make a last ditch effort to proclaim the gospel of Jesus Christ throughout the world. Thus, as the Lord sent out His twelve Apostles to preach His gospel unto the house of Israel during His ministry on earth; in like manner, the Lord shall send out another group of special servants to preach His gospel during the last days. However, instead of just twelve individuals, the Lord shall multiply this number by twelve thousand for a total of *144,000*. Though this force shall be greater in number than their predecessors, their marching orders from the Lord shall be the same: *"Behold, I send you forth as sheep in the midst of wolves: be ye therefore wise as serpents, and harmless as doves. But beware of men: for they will deliver you up to the councils, and they will scourge you in their synagogues; And ye shall be brought before governors and kings for my sake, for a testimony against them and the Gentiles. But when they deliver you up, take no thought how or what ye shall speak: for it shall be given*

---

13. Isaiah 29:11-24

you in that same hour what ye shall speak. For it is not ye that speak, but the Spirit of your Father which speaketh in you. And the brother shall deliver up the brother to death, and the father the child: and the children shall rise up against their parents, and cause them to be put to death. And ye shall be hated of all men for my name's sake: but he that endureth to the end shall be saved. But when they persecute you in this city, flee ye into another: for verily I say unto you, Ye shall not have gone over the cities of Israel, till the Son of man be come."[14]

Eventually, this missionary effort will be curtailed due to intense persecution, and the *144,000* shall receive their reward. This is when the times of the Gentiles will be fulfilled.[15] This is when God shall begin to unleash His wrath upon the earth. This is the event that John saw when he observed a great earthquake, sun turning black, moon become as blood, and stars fall from the heavens, and all this shall occur just prior to the sounding of the seventh trumpet as discussed in chapter 11.

> *12 And I beheld when he had opened the sixth seal, and, lo, there was a great earthquake; and the sun became black as sackcloth of hair, and the moon became as blood;*
> *13 And the stars of heaven fell unto the earth, even as a fig tree casteth her untimely figs, when she is shaken of a mighty wind.*
> *14 And the heaven departed as a scroll when it is rolled together; and every mountain and island were moved out of their places.*
> *15 And the kings of the earth, and the great men, and the rich men, and the chief captains, and the mighty men, and every bondman, and every free man, hid themselves in the dens and in the rocks of the mountains;*

---

14. Matt. 10:16-23
15. Luke 21:24

16 And said to the mountains and rocks, Fall on us, and hide us from the face of him that sitteth on the throne, and from the wrath of the Lamb:
17 For the great day of his wrath is come; and who shall be able to stand?[16]

---

16. Rev. 6:12-17

7

Missionary Effort in the Sixth Seal

Apparently, this last ditch effort by the *144,000*, to bring as many as shall come to the Church of Jesus Christ, is extremely important because the angel is willing to provide more information concerning this subject.

What was the angel, who ascending from the east, tasked to accomplish?

Since the missionary effort involving the *144,000* servants of God shall extend into the seventh seal, or twenty-first century, this angel has been tasked with the authority to ensure that the angels of the sixth seal (who have the power to unleash the wrath of God) do *not* allow this to happen until the *144,000*, upon completion of their missions, have been sealed (sanctified by the Spirit) to inherit eternal life and exaltation.

> *1 And after these things I saw four angels standing on the four corners of the earth, holding the four winds of the earth, that the wind should not blow on the earth, nor on the sea, nor on any tree.*
>
> *2 And I saw another angel ascending from the east, having the seal of the living God: and he cried with a loud voice to the four angels, to whom it was given to hurt the earth and the sea,*
>
> *3 Saying, Hurt not the earth, neither the sea, nor the trees, till we have sealed the servants of our God in their foreheads.[1]*

Who will be involved in this missionary effort?

Individuals from each of the twelve tribes of Israel (except Dan) shall be ordained to carry the gospel to the seekers of truth. More details concerning this task shall be given in chapter 14.

> *4 And I heard the number of them which were sealed: and there were sealed an hundred and forty and four thousand of all the tribes of the children of Israel.*
>
> *5 Of the tribe of Juda were sealed twelve thousand. Of the tribe of Reuben were sealed twelve thousand. Of the tribe of Gad were sealed twelve thousand.*
>
> *6 Of the tribe of Aser were sealed twelve thousand. Of the tribe of Nepthalim were sealed twelve thousand. Of the tribe of Manasses were sealed twelve thousand.*
>
> *7 Of the tribe of Simeon were sealed twelve thousand. Of the tribe of Levi were sealed twelve thousand. Of the tribe of Issachar were sealed twelve thousand.*
>
> *8 Of the tribe of Zabulon were sealed twelve thousand. Of the tribe of Joseph were sealed twelve thousand. Of the tribe of Benjamin were sealed twelve thousand.[2]*

---

1. Rev. 7:1-3
2. Rev. 7:4-8

How successful is this missionary effort?

Eventually, this overall missionary effort (accomplished by the general membership of the Church *and* the *144,000*) shall be so successful that great multitudes of people from all nations shall be gathered before God the Father and Jesus Christ to receive white robes as a symbol of their faithfulness. This is why, in a show of love for all that the Father and Son had done for them, an out-pouring of appreciation shall be heard emanating from this great multitude.

> 9 *After this I beheld, and, lo, a great multitude, which no man could number, of all nations, and kindreds, and people, and tongues, stood before the throne, and before the Lamb, clothed with white robes, and palms in their hands;*
>
> *10 And cried with a loud voice, saying, Salvation to our God which sitteth upon the throne, and unto the Lamb.*
>
> *11 And all the angels stood round about the throne, and about the elders and the four beasts, and fell before the throne on their faces, and worshipped God,*
>
> *12 Saying, Amen: Blessing, and glory, and wisdom, and thanksgiving, and honour, and power, and might, be unto our God for ever and ever. Amen.*[3]

What is the significance of the white robes?

The white robes symbolize purity and righteousness.[4] They are given to those faithful Saints who purify their lives through the Atonement of Jesus Christ, as determined by their willingness to obey His commandments and remain true and faithful to their covenants. These are they who remain true to the word even when subjected to great tribulation, even unto death.

---

3. Rev. 7:9-12
4. Rev. 19-8

13 And one of the elders answered, saying unto me, What are these which are arrayed in white robes? and whence came they?

14 And I said unto him, Sir, thou knowest. And he said to me, These are they which came out of great tribulation, and have washed their robes, and made them white in the blood of the Lamb.

15 Therefore are they before the throne of God, and serve him day and night in his temple: and he that sitteth on the throne shall dwell among them.

16 They shall hunger no more, neither thirst any more; neither shall the sun light on them, nor any heat.

17 For the Lamb which is in the midst of the throne shall feed them, and shall lead them unto living fountains of waters: and God shall wipe away all tears from their eyes.[5]

---

5. Rev. 7:13-17

8

Seventh Seal, First – Fourth Trumpets

J ust the knowledge that a worldwide missionary effort shall bring multitudes of individuals to God should lift the spirit of any prophet, nevertheless, any joy John may have experienced would be severely dampened by the news he shall soon receive; for John is about to see what is behind the door of the seventh seal, which is from 2000 A.D. to 3000 A.D.

The period from 2000 A.D., until the Second Coming of Jesus Christ, shall be a time of great tribulation. Great fear shall come upon all mankind, with wars and rumors of wars, and nations fighting against nations. It shall be a time when false christ's and false prophets arise, and when the love of men shall wax cold. It shall be a time of famines, pestilences, and earthquakes. In short, it will be a time when many souls, unless they repent and heed the warnings given by the Lord, shall be released to the cunning wiles of the adversary. Just the thought of what shall happen in the future arouses many questions, such as: Will the

Saints really have to worry? Is the battle between the Lord and Satan still being waged; if so, who is winning? What will happen to the followers of Christ? How does one protect oneself? And how does a person know when the Second Coming is near? Is there an answer to these questions? The response is yes; it was given (by a loving Savior) for the benefit of all mankind approximately thirty-four hundred years ago.

It was at this time when a very peculiar battle took place between the mighty men of Jericho and the children of God. This would be known as the battle of Jericho. Prior to the start of this conflict, the Lord informed Joshua, that if he followed some very specific commands he would be victorious and the city and its inhabitants would be given into his hands. Joshua was then instructed to have his men carry the Ark of the Covenant (as the priests sounded their trumpets) around the city once each day for six consecutive days. However, on the seventh day they were to march around the city not once, but seven times then, at the sound of the trump, give a loud shout and the city walls would come tumbling down.

Prior to this battle, Joshua ordered his military not to take any spoils of war, except only that consecrated by the Lord. He also directed certain soldiers (at the start of hostilities) to protect Rahab and her family from destruction. This is because Rahab (the harlot) and her family had earlier shielded the spies of Joshua while they were secretly conducting surveillance within the walls of Jericho. When the appointed time arrived, Joshua's army conducted the battle as previously described. After his soldiers completed the seventh cycle of the city, on the seventh day, at the sound of the trumpet the men gave a shout and the walls of the city fell to the ground; they then invaded the city, killed the inhabitants (with the exception of Rahab and her family) and burned everything with fire.[1] However, the Lord was displeased with Joshua and his men because an individual by the name of Achan, instead of heeding divine instruction, had appropriated for himself a Babylonian type garment and some silver and gold. As punishment, Achan, his family, and all their possessions were destroyed and burned with fire.[2]

But, how is the battle of Jericho a precursor of what shall transpire from 2000 A.D. until the Second Coming of the Lord? This battle is a type and shadow of the events leading to the return of the King of Kings and Lord of Lords. For example: As the battle for Jericho was conducted between the army of Joshua and the mighty men of Jericho; the battle concerning good and evil is conducted between the army of Christ and the minions of Satan. Just as the Lord told Joshua that Jericho would be given into his hands; the followers of Christ have been divinely informed that Satan shall be given into the hands of the Lord. As the Ark of the Covenant symbolized the presence, sanction, and support of Jehovah; the Saints, in the last days, can expect to receive the companionship, approval, and help from the Savior. As the men of Joshua (at the sounding of a trumpet) were told to circle the city once each day for six days, in order to give the inhabitants of Jericho a chance to avoid bloodshed and death; in like manner, John was informed that six angels will soon sound their trumpets for six consecutive times, in order to give the population of the world a chance to repent and avoid a spiritual death. As Joshua was told that on the seventh day he was to circle the city seven times and then sound the trumpet as a sign for his army to dispense his wrath upon Jericho; similarly, John was informed that a seventh angel shall sound his trumpet as a signal for seven other angels to dispense their vials of God's wrath upon Babylon (the wicked). As Joshua was directed to destroy Jericho and burn everything with fire (except that which was covered by divine protection); in like manner, at the Second

---

1. Joshua 6:22-25
2. Joshua 7:18-26

Coming, Babylon shall be destroyed by fire (except that which is covered by divine decree). As the army of Joshua was protected (in front and behind) by a group of Special Forces; the Lord shall protect His Saints (in front and behind) by a special contingent of angels as the wrath of God is dispensed upon the wicked. As Rahab (the harlot) was rewarded for helping the spies of Joshua accomplish their duties; the Gentiles of the world (during the last days) shall be rewarded for helping the Saints in their hour of need. As Achan, his family, and all their possessions were destroyed and burned with fire for not heeding the word of God; all who side with the adversary, by taking on the mark of the beast, shall be destroyed and burned with fire for disobeying the word of God.

In sum, the reason the battle of Jericho was fought under such unusual constraints is to provide hope and understanding of how Christ (at the end of days) shall overthrow Babylon and defeat the adversary. Additionally, the seven trumpets and seven plagues will act as a yardstick in determining how much time is left before the Second Coming occurs. Each time the army of Joshua marched around Jericho, it meant that time was running out for the inhabitants therein. Each time an angel sounds his trumpet, it means that time is spiraling down for the nations of the earth. But, how do we know when an angel (in heaven) sounds his trumpet? When a trumpet sounds, a corresponding event shall occur in the sky and on earth. As each bowl of wrath is dispensed, a related action shall take place in the heavens and on this planet. This is the key that shall enable the Saints to decipher the signs of the times and know when the Lord's Second Coming is at the door.

What happened when John opened the seventh seal?

He witnesses the main event that shall take place during the period 2000 A.D. until the final coming of Jesus Christ.

As the seventh seal is opened, John sees that *there is silence in the heaven for about half an hour.* It is important to understand the meaning of the term *"about half an hour"* because it indicates how much time shall elapse following the year 2000 A.D. until the serious devastations concerning the seven trumpets begin to occur. In this case, the *"about half an hour"* equates to about 21 months.

The Lord has told his prophets that whenever he gives a vision or figure of any kind, He holds Himself responsible to give us the interpretation. In chapter 13, John is shown an event that mentions the beast. Initially, this event is described as lasting 42 months.[3] Later, the same event is depicted as lasting one hour,[4] therefore, it follows that one hour equals 42 months, or one half hour is 21 months.

> *1 And when he had opened the seventh seal, there was silence in heaven about the space of half an hour.*[5]

After the half hour period expired, what did John see?

He identifies seven angels who are preparing to sound their trumpets. The sounding of the trumpet proclaims a coming judgment. It should also be noted that these angels have been given powers over certain parts of elements of the earth and universe to either save or destroy life, as we know it.

> *2 And I saw the seven angels which stood before God; and to them were given seven trumpets.*

---

3. Rev. 13:4-7
4. Rev. 17:12-14
5. Rev. 8:1

3 And another angel came and stood at the altar, having a golden censer; and there was given unto him much incense, that he should offer it with the prayers of all saints upon the golden altar which was before the throne.

4 And the smoke of the incense, which came with the prayers of the saints, ascended up before God out of the angel's hand.

5 And the angel took the censer, and filled it with fire of the altar, and cast it into the earth: and there were voices, and thunderings, and lightnings, and an earthquake.

6 And the seven angels which had the seven trumpets prepared themselves to sound.[6]

When the first angel sounds, what will happen?

The angel who sounds this trumpet has been given power over the earth, thus when John sees, as it were, hail fall from the sky, followed by fire and bloodshed, it provides an ominous vision of what shall occur.

On September 11, 2001, approximately 21 months after the turn of the twenty-first century, the Twin Towers in New York were attacked by terrorists bent on destroying this country. This attack took place during a beautiful autumn morning when two commercial airliners were intentionally flown by highjackers into the twin skyscrapers located near Battery Park. As great clouds of black smoke started billowing skyward, shards of glass mingled with pieces of concrete and blood began hailing down upon the unsuspecting pedestrians walking far below.

This incident marks the starting point whereby over the period of many years, various disasters, in the form of earthquakes, tornadoes, fires, and war shall increasingly rage until a third part of the earths' trees shall be burned, along with all the green grass. Much of humanity is already aware that something

---

6. Rev. 8:2-6

is happening, and that the world is becoming a more danger-
ous place in which to live. Some individuals have attempted to
explain away this phenomenon as global warming, while others
have said that the earth is just passing through a cyclical event
that normally occurs over a long period. Interestingly, no one is
willing to accept the notion that this change is caused by a loving God informing His children that *now* is the time to repent.

> 7 *The first angel sounded, and there followed hail and fire
> mingled with blood, and they were cast upon the earth:
> and the third part of trees was burnt up, and all green
> grass was burnt up.*[7]

What did John see when the second angel blew his trumpet?

This angel has been given power over the sea, therefore,
when John observes a great burning mountain cast into the sea
resulting in the death of much sea life and the destruction of
many ships, it provides a foreboding description of an event that
shall initiate a time when increasing destruction shall be poured
out upon the seas and oceans of the world.

During the night of December 30, 2002, a volcano on the
island of Stromboli, Italy, erupted with such force that numerous car-size boulders were catapulted into the air and large
sections of the mountain slid into the sea. The tsunami (giant
wave) created by this eruption tore boats from their anchors,
damaged many houses, and forced an evacuation of all its island
inhabitants to Sicily. This volcanic event put the world on notice that hurricanes, tsunami's, earthquakes, and environmental
poisoning, will continue to escalate until a third part of sea life
is destroyed.

---

7. Rev. 8:7

8 And the second angel sounded, and as it were a great mountain burning with fire was cast into the sea: and the third part of the sea became blood;

9 And the third part of the creatures which were in the sea, and had life, died; and the third part of the ships were destroyed.[8]

At the sound of the third trumpet, what happened?

This third angel holds power over the rivers and fountains of the earth. Consequently, when John sees a great star falling from heaven *(burning like a lamp)* it symbolizes the beginning of when (over time) many shall die from the pollution of our streams, rivers, and lakes.

At 6:23 A.M., on February 1, 2003, a bright light was observed streaking across the heavens, appearing as a great star. This bright light was the space ship Columbia returning to earth. However, on this pre-dawn morning, the image was much brighter than normal, the result of something that had gone terribly wrong. A catastrophic event had caused the spaceship to begin breaking apart as it entered the atmosphere high above the California coast. It then began raining debris over a thousand miles of countryside far below. When the spacecraft started to come apart over California, it was *glowing like a lamp.* As it continued to streak toward Florida, parts fell off over the lakes, rivers and springs of several different states. Finally, just prior to reaching the Arkansas border, the main body of the shuttle separated into hundreds of smaller pieces. God did not cause this event to occur, but the worldwide attention it received, made it possible to be used as a sign that a change needs to take place to avoid the destruction that is reserved for the wicked.

---

8. Rev. 8:8-9

10 And the third angel sounded, and there fell a great star
from heaven, burning as it were a lamp, and it fell upon the
third part of the rivers, and upon the fountains of waters;
11 And the name of the star is called Wormwood: and the
third part of the waters became wormwood; and many
men died of the waters, because they were made bitter.[9]

What was depicted when the fourth angel sounded?

This fourth angel has been given power over fire; thus this prophecy implies that something in the atmosphere shall interfere with the light coming from the sun, moon, and stars, and that this interference shall occur over a large part of the earth.

In the March 2003 issue of the *National Geographic Magazine*, there is an article titled, "Toxic Storms Choke Asia."[10] This article informs the reader of massive toxic storms that descend upon the inhabitants of China, Japan, and North and South Korea each spring, bringing with it multiple amounts of toxic pollutants. These toxic storms are the result of overgrazed grasslands, dry lakebeds, factories, emissions from vehicles and the burning of coal, weeds, wood, and cow dung.[11] These storms have become an annual event. Normally they would arrive in April, but are now coming earlier with more intensity. In 2002, they began to range beyond the borders of Asia, reaching across the Pacific Ocean and edging into California. A study pointed out that these storms are responsible for drastically altering rainfall patterns, making acid rain, damaging crops and trees, and threatening hundreds of thousands of people with respiratory disease.[12] Though the storms have been growing for several years, the world was not aware of the magnitude of this danger until it was published in the March 2003 issue of the *National Geographic Magazine*. If men do not heed the warning voice

---

9. Rev. 8:10, 11
10. *National Geographic*, "Toxic Storms Choke Asia," March 2003, Geographic, Weather Section
11. Yahoo News, A Darkening Sky, U.S. News & World Report, March 10, 2003
12. Asian Brown Cloud poses global threat. (The Facts) CNN. Com/WORLD, August 12, 2002

of this angel, then many individuals are doomed to experience an early death from an increasingly polluted atmosphere caused from the effects of man and nature.

> *12 And the fourth angel sounded, and the third part of the sun was smitten, and the third part of the moon, and the third part of the stars; so as the third part of them was darkened, and the day shone not for a third part of it, and the night likewise.[13]*

What does it mean when the angel says "Woe, woe, woe to the inhabiters of the earth"?

The word *woe* refers to intense suffering. Therefore, when the fifth, sixth, and seventh angels sound, it will signify that something is about to happen that shall cause extreme suffering to those involved.

> *13 And I beheld, and heard an angel flying through the midst of heaven, saying with a loud voice, Woe, woe, woe, to the inhabiters of the earth by reason of the other voices of the trumpet of the three angels, which are yet to sound![14]*

---

13. Rev. 8:12
14. Rev. 8:13

9

The Fifth & Sixth Trumpets

Until now, the visions presented to John concerned how divine intervention will affect the earth, oceans, rivers, and light coming from the sun, moon, and stars.

It is important to know that the angel who shall sound the fifth trump has been given power over the sealing of the servants of God, and for the committing or taking away of the everlasting gospel of Jesus Christ.[1] Additionally, he has the duty to warn the world of what shall occur if they reject the gospel. Moreover, if they shall not repent, he is tasked with the responsibility to prepare the way for their destruction. John is now shown where the final conflict will begin and how it shall spread until all nations are at war.

What event will take place at the sounding of the fifth trumpet?

---

1. Rev. 7:2, 3

As the fifth angel sounds his trump, John sees a star (angel) fall from heaven to earth. This angel is given a key, which he uses to open the bottomless pit.

> *1 And the fifth angel sounded, and I saw a star fall from heaven unto the earth: and to him was given the key of the bottomless pit.*
> *2 And he opened the bottomless pit; and there arose a smoke out of the pit, as the smoke of a great furnace; and the sun and the air were darkened by reason of the smoke of the pit.*[2]

From the smoke that arose out of the pit, what came forth?

When the pit is opened, a sinister force is released upon all humanity. As this force expands, it soon becomes apparent that what John sees is a vast army of armored equipment (locust) moving into position for battle.

> *3 And there came out of the smoke locusts upon the earth: and unto them was given power, as the scorpions of the earth have power.*[3]

How will this battle be different from all the rest?

During this conflict no damage shall be done to the earth, no one will die, and it shall last only five months. Yet those men who have not the seal of God in their forehead, shall be tormented (as if stung by a scorpion) so excruciatingly that they will wish to die, but their desire shall not be granted.

---

2. Rev. 9:1, 2
3. Rev. 9:3

*4 And it was commanded them that they should not hurt
the grass of the earth, neither any green thing, neither any
tree; but only those men which have not the seal of God
in their foreheads.*

*5 And to them it was given that they should not kill them,
but that they should be tormented five months: and their
torment was as the torment of a scorpion, when he striketh
a man.*

*6 And in those days shall men seek death, and shall not find
it; and shall desire to die, and death shall flee from them.*[4]

How could a battle with so many unusual restraints ever occur?

On March 17, 2003, President George W. Bush, during a national televised speech, told Saddam Hussein his time was finished, and that he had to either flee Iraq or face war.[5] This moment marked the end of a five-month psychological war that the United States and its allies had waged against Saddam's Iraq regime in hopes of persuading the dictator to refrain from training terrorists and to renounce the use of weapons of mass destruction.

This psychological war was the result of many attempts to rein in a dictator bent on conquering his neighbors. In 1979, Saddam instigated a coup and became the leader of Iraq. In 1980, he invaded Iran, then, ten years later; he tried to annex the oil fields of Kuwait. This prompted the United States to join with coalition forces, to force Saddam out of Kuwait. Following this, the dictator gassed thousands of his own fellow citizens to quell a suspected uprising. During the ensuing years, numerous United Nations restrictions were placed on Saddam. In spite of these efforts, he continued to build his arsenals of weapons, and initiated a program to finance terrorist activities

---

4. Rev. 9:4-6
5. Bush Tells Saddam: Flee Iraq or Face War, Yahoo News.com 3/17/2003

bent on destroying Israel. Following the Twin Towers attack in 2001, the United States, along with many other countries, went to war against countries that supported terrorist organizations. The initial intention was not to topple Saddam's regime but to curtail his militaristic aggression. However, once diplomatic negotiations became impossible, decisions were made to mobilize forces, as if going to war, and hope that Saddam would see the futility and acquiesce to allied demands. The psychological war began when President Bush signed a congressional resolution on October 16, 2002. The psychological war ended five months later on March 16, 2003, when President Bush met with the British Prime Minister Tony Blair, and his counter part, Jose Mari Asnar, on the Azores islands. There, it was determined that Saddam would not change and that any hope for a diplomatic solution was futile.[6]

Thus, what actually happened compares very closely with what John sees, in that, during the conflict no damage is done to the earth, no one dies, and it lasts only 5 months (October 16, 2002, to March 16, 2003). Even the description of how only those men not under God's seal of protection are tormented (as if stung by a scorpion) is accurate. This is because the symptoms generated from a scorpion sting are, pain, anxiety, sweating, chills, numbness, nausea, tightness in chest, shortness of breath, and a general feeling of imminent death. The general symptoms of a panic attack are very much the same.[7] Those individuals most susceptible to this affliction would be they who had committed crimes against humanity. Because of these crimes, the fear of capture, torture, and death would be almost overwhelming, and ironically, the more serious the crimes, the worse the panic attacks.

---

6. http://www.rte.ie/news/2003/0316/iraq.html
7. http://me.essortment.com/panicattacksym_rhio.htm

What evidence is there to indicate that the locust John describes is the weaponry of a vast army?

When attempting to depict the locusts, John compares their images to that of horses, lions, and scorpions with breastplates of iron. In other words, to the untrained eye a tank painted to blend in with the desert sands resembles a lion. A missile, angled skyward from its launching platform, is similar to a giant scorpion. Moreover, when John says the sound of their wings is as the sound of chariots of many horses running to battle, it is easy to imagine the sound of helicopter gun ships flying into battle.

> 7 And the shapes of the locusts were like unto horses prepared unto battle; and on their heads were as it were crowns like gold, and their faces were as the faces of men.
> 8 And they had hair as the hair of women, and their teeth were as the teeth of lions.
> 9 And they had breastplates, as it were breastplates of iron; and the sound of their wings was as the sound of chariots of many horses running to battle.
> 10 And they had tails like unto scorpions, and there were stings in their tails: and their power was to hurt men five months.[8]

Who is the ultimate commander of the evil side of this vast army?

The behind-the-scenes commander, shown to John, is "Abaddon" (Destroyer), which is one of the titles attributed to Satan. He is the commander of all forces who seek to war against the followers of Christ.

---

8. Rev. 9:7-10

11 And they had a king over them, which is the angel of the bottomless pit, whose name in the Hebrew tongue is Abaddon, but in the Greek tongue hath his name Apollyon.[9]

What will happen when the sixth angel sounds?

With the sounding of the sixth trumpet, John hears a voice directing that all restraining devices (holding back the tide of war) be released. In other words, God is removing all barriers and shall allow the war to escalate to a point where eventually a third part of men shall be killed by fire, smoke, and sulfur. This is to be expected because the angel who sounds the sixth trumpet is the one who has been given power to pronounce a verdict once a judgment has been decided.

12 One woe is past; and, behold, there come two woes more hereafter.
13 And the sixth angel sounded, and I heard a voice from the four horns of the golden altar which is before God,
14 Saying to the sixth angel which had the trumpet, Loose the four angels which are bound in the great river Euphrates.
15 And the four angels were loosed, which were prepared for an hour, and a day, and a month, and a year, for to slay the third part of men.[10]

How will the actual fighting begin?

On March 20, 2003, plums of sulfur and smoke began lighting up the early morning skies over Baghdad as U.S. and coalition forces began bombing Iraq.[11] Within hours, armored vehicles began rumbling forth to engage the enemy. The next day, newspapers around the world proclaimed, "WAR BEGINS." Other news agencies noted that this was first major, multi-national

---

9. Rev. 9:11
10. Rev. 9:12-15
11. U.S. launches cruise missiles at Saddam. CNN. Com/world, March 20, 2003

war of the twenty-first century. Though this conflict starts out relatively small, the way is now open whereby many nations, through treaties and entangled alliances, shall be drawn into war.

> *16 And the number of the army of the horsemen were two hundred thousand thousand: and I heard the number of them.*
>
> *17 And thus I saw the horses in the vision, and them that sat on them, having breastplates of fire, and of jacinth, and brimstone: and the heads of the horses were as the heads of lions; and out of their mouths issued fire and smoke and brimstone.*
>
> *18 By these three was the third part of men killed, by the fire, and by the smoke, and by the brimstone, which issued out of their mouths.*
>
> *19 For their power is in their mouth, and in their tails: for their tails were like unto serpents, and had heads, and with them they do hurt.[12]*

As war begins to spread, will humanity ever recognize the real reasons why this is happening and change their ways?

Sadly, John is told, as devastating as these wars are, men still shall not repent.

> *20 And the rest of the men which were not killed by these plagues yet repented not of the works of their hands, that they should not worship devils, and idols of gold, and silver, and brass, and stone, and of wood: which neither can see, nor hear, nor walk:*
>
> *21 Neither repented they of their murders, nor of their sorceries, nor of their fornication, nor of their thefts.[13]*

---

12. Rev. 9:16-19
13. Rev. 9:20-21

10

The Mission of John

After being shown that war shall eventually consume a third part of humanity, the time is ready for John to receive an important assignment. This is significant because this chapter deals with the period of time that shall soon take place in our day. In this chapter, a mighty angel appears to John. This angel has the power to control the elements of the earth and can determine how much time is allocated to a particular operation before declaring, *It is done*, and thus move on to another part of the Lord's plan. The mission of this mighty angel is to give John a small book that contains some very important information that John (in the last days) shall unfold to the eyes of all the world.

Who is this mighty angel?

His name is Michael the archangel.[1] He has great power over the world, as indicated by having one foot on the earth and

---

1. Dan. 10:21; 12:1; 10:13-14

one foot on the seas. He is sometimes heard saying the words, *"It is finished,"* or *"It is done."*[2] He has also been give power to carry out the verdict, once a judgment has been determined.

> *1 And I saw another mighty angel come down from heaven, clothed with a cloud: and a rainbow was upon his head, and his face was as it were the sun, and his feet as pillars of fire:*
> *2 And he had in his hand a little book open: and he set his right foot upon the sea, and his left foot on the earth,*[3]

What did Michael say?

When Michael gives an order, the seven thunders respond, but what they say is not revealed. Knowing that Michael is making this declaration provides an ominous foreboding of what shall occur.

> *3 And cried with a loud voice, as when a lion roareth: and when he had cried, seven thunders uttered their voices.*
> *4 And when the seven thunders had uttered their voices, I was about to write: and I heard a voice from heaven saying unto me, Seal up those things which the seven thunders uttered, and write them not.*[4]

Is there some indication of what to expect when the seven thunders utter their voices?

What Michael does once the seven thunders utter their voices, provides an important clue concerning what shall happen. After addressing the seven thunders, Michael makes a solemn pledge to God that the time restraints, which have been placed upon the heavens, earth, and seas, shall no longer exist.

---

2. Rev. 10:7
3. Rev. 10:1, 2
4. Rev. 10:3, 4

As previously mentioned in chapter 6, the Lord has restrained the angels from harming the earth until a missionary effort to the Gentiles has been fulfilled. Once this is accomplished, Michael is compelled to declare that these restraints no longer apply, and thus, is obligated to order the seven thunders to begin dispensing the wrath of God upon the earth.

But how can one be assured that this is the correct interpretation, and that the wrath spoken of here is not the wrath that shall occur just before the Second Coming? This is evident because after Michael declares, *"there should be time no longer"* (thus indicating it was time for the seven thunders to act) he goes on to say, *"But in the days of the voice of the seventh angel, when he shall begin to sound, the mystery of God should be finished,"* thereby implying that the actions of the seven thunders shall be completed before the seventh trumpet sounds, and, as outlined in chapter 14, there are many events that must still take place after the seventh angel trumpets his horn.

> 5 *And the angel which I saw stand upon the sea and upon the earth lifted up his hand to heaven,*
>
> 6 *And sware by him that liveth for ever and ever, who created heaven, and the things that therein are, and the earth, and the things that therein are, and the sea, and the things which are therein, that there should be time no longer:*[5]
>
> 7 *But in the days of the voice of the seventh angel, when he shall begin to sound, the mystery of God should be finished, as he hath declared to his servants the prophets.*[6]

---

5. Rev. 10: 5, 6
6. Rev. 10:7

When he gave John the little book, what did the angel ask him to do?

He is told to eat it, and that in his mouth it would be sweet as honey, yet in his stomach, it would be very bitter. The book is sweet because it outlines the blessings God has in store for those who follow His commandments; and it is bitter because it describes the terrible calamites that will befall those who shall not repent and follow His teachings. John is then told that the time shall come when he would again prophesy before many people.

> 8 And the voice which I heard from heaven spake unto me again, and said, Go and take the little book which is open in the hand of the angel which standeth upon the sea and upon the earth.
>
> 9 And I went unto the angel, and said unto him, Give me the little book. And he said unto me, Take it, and eat it up; and it shall make thy belly bitter, but it shall be in thy mouth sweet as honey.
>
> 10 And I took the little book out of the angel's hand, and ate it up; and it was in my mouth sweet as honey: and as soon as I had eaten it, my belly was bitter.
>
> 11 And he said unto me, Thou must prophesy again before many peoples, and nations, and tongues, and kings.[7]

---

7. Rev. 10:8-11

11

The Sixth Trumpet Continued

After John receives the information that he would, *again*, have the opportunity to prophesy before many people, he is given a reed to measure something very curious.

He is told to measure the temple of God, the altar, and those who worship therein. But the court outside the temple must be left out, because it is given unto the Gentiles, and they shall tread the holy city (Jerusalem) under foot for forty-two months. Thus, the angel is indicating to John that a temple is being measured for Jerusalem and, following the construction of this temple, the Gentiles shall tread this city under foot for three and a half years.

John now sees two witnesses arriving in Jerusalem with authority from heaven to testify of Jesus Christ. These two prophets shall have power to control the elements of nature in order to keep their enemies at bay until they have accomplished their mission.

When their work is complete, the adversary's demonic cohorts shall slay them and leave their bodies in the streets of Jerusalem for three and a half days. Subsequently, a great miracle shall occur. In response to a voice from on high, these two witnesses shall rise from the dead and ascend to heaven. Next, a great earthquake shall shake the land causing much death and destruction.

How does one know that the term "to measure" is associated with building a house (temple) for the Lord?

Zechariah witnessed something similar to what John saw when he learned that prior to the Second Coming, Jerusalem would be measured in order to build a house for the Lord. This is so the Lord would have a place to dwell in the midst of His people.[1]

The building of this temple should not come as a surprise. For Daniel was informed that, in the last days, a covenant concerning the children of Israel would be confirmed for one week.[2] In this covenant, God made a promise to Abraham that the time should come when his seed would gather to the land of Jerusalem, to receive the opportunity to be reconciled to Jesus Christ.[3] In this case, *"one week"* is a Biblical term meaning *seven years*.

It should be noted that this temple is *not* the temple that the Jews expect to build on their holy temple mount. We know this because Ezekiel was informed that once that specific temple is built, it would never be defiled.[4] Whereas, the holy sanctuary (temple), depicted here, shall be defiled and trodden underfoot.[5] When shall this temple be built? As *seventy years* elapsed while the children of Judah were held captive under the rule of Nebuchadnezzar, in like manner, at least *seventy years* must also

---

1. Zech. 1:16; 2:1-5, 11, 12
2. Dan. 9:27 (In Biblical terms, one week can equate to seven years)
3. Gen. 12:1-3: Isa. 44:21, 22, 26, Dan. 9:24, Psalm 102:28; Ezek. 37:12-26
4. Ezek. 43:4-12
5. Dan. 8:11-14

pass from the re-birth of Israel until a house for the Lord shall *again* grace the hills of Jerusalem.

How did Israel, initially, become estranged from God? In the book of Exodus we find the following words, *"For in six days the LORD made heaven and earth, the sea, and all that in them is, and rested the seventh day: wherefore the LORD blessed the sabbath day, and hallowed it."*[6] After our first parents were expelled from the Garden of Eden, they had to work by the sweat of their brow for food, clothing, and shelter. The Lord knew that they would need to rest periodically from their daily labor; therefore, He established a plan that followed the same pattern He used when creating the heavens and the earth. This plan called for the seventh day of each week to be set aside as a day of rest and renewal, and was to be called the Sabbath day. However, instead of being just a day of rest from physical labor, it was also a day for the rejuvenation of body, mind, and spirit; a day where one could come closer to God by contemplating past, present, and future actions, and take the necessary steps to reconcile any differences. As an individual begins to sin on a continuous basis, the desire to use the Sabbath day to reconcile with the will of God becomes increasingly remote, until, eventually, it disappears altogether. The same is true, whether it's a single person or a nation of people.

If a nation goes astray, how does God rectify the situation? A perfect example of what He does is found in the book of Daniel. During the reign of Jehoiakim (king of Judah) the children of Judah had drifted so far from the teachings of the prophets, that God allowed Nebuchadnezzar, king of Babylon, to sack Jerusalem, destroy the holy temple, and carry the people off to Babylon. To accomplish the reconciliation, God used *time* as His primary instrument of choice. The Lord decreed, through His prophet Jeremiah, that Judah must spend *seventy years* in

---

6. Exodus 20:11

captivity as a result of their evil doings.[7] Eventually, the hearts of the children of Judah were softened, as they came to realize that all their hardships were the result of disobedience in doing God's will. Once the Lord had achieved His goal; He forgave the children of Judah, restored them to their beloved city, and reconstructed their temple, with the assistance of Cyrus, king of Persia.[8]

How does this knowledge help us to know when the temple, referred to in Revelation chapter 11, will be built? This information, concerning how the children of Judah were taken captive during the time of Nebuchadnezzar, is a type and shadow of what shall happen to the Jewish people in the last days. For example, following the crucifixion of the Messiah, the Jews had drifted so far from the teachings of the prophets, that God (as previously mentioned) allowed Titus, commander of the Roman army, to sack Jerusalem, destroy the holy temple, and disperse the Jews throughout the entire world.[9] Eventually, after undergoing tremendous suffering for approximately 1878 years, the Lord opened a way whereby the Jewish people could return to their ancestral homeland. The Lord specifically states that this return did *not* happen because the Jews had harkened unto His words, but because He said *He* would do it, and the Lord Almighty is always true to His word.[10]

For reconciliation to work, the Jews shall be given *seventy years* from the re-birth of their nation in 1948, to prepare themselves. How do we know this is an accurate summation? The Lord told Jeremiah, *"And I will cause the captivity of Judah and the captivity of Israel to return, and will build them, as at the first. And I will cleanse them from all their iniquity, whereby they have sinned against me; and I will pardon all their iniquities, whereby they have sinned, and whereby they have transgressed against me."*[11] From this information, the sequence of how the

---

7. See 2 Chron. 36:21   10. Jer. 33:7-9
8. Ezra 1:1-3   11. Jer. 33:7, 8
9. See Matt. 24:2-21

Lord shall reconcile with His people is clearly visible. This process shall emulate the pattern of the return and reconciliation of Judah from Babylon. This is evident when the Lord told Jeremiah *"And I will cause the captivity of Judah and the captivity of Israel to return, and will build them, as at the first."*[12] Thus, the words *"as at first"* indicate that He shall cause the captivity of the Jews to return and be reconciled, as He did when Judah returned from Babylon. This reconciliation pattern shall involve a *seventy-year* wait, building of a holy temple, and an invitation to return to a fellowship with God. The only difference between the return of Judah from Babylon, as compared to the Jewish return in the last days, is that the former, did not have to experience a worldwide dispersion, because they were *not* involved with the death of their Messiah.

It should be noted, that the words *"as at first"* not only applies to the *captivity of Judah*, but also to the captivity of Israel as previously discussed in chapter 6. This latter group will be of special interest to scholars around the world because these are none other than the main portion of the *"Lost Ten Tribes of Israel."* This time of reconciliation is when they shall make their appearance from the land of the North. These are also they who will provide the missionaries that shall comprise the majority of the *144,000*. This is important to know so steps can be taken to prepare for their arrival in Zion.[13]

Thus, at least *seventy years* must pass before a house for the Lord can be built in Jerusalem. In preparation for this event, the Lord shall stir up the hearts of those individuals who can cause this to happen; much as when He stirred up the spirit of Cyrus, king of Persia, to build the holy temple in Jerusalem following the Jewish captivity at the hands of Nebuchadnezzar.[14]

---

12. Jer. 33:7
13. See 2 Kings 17:6, 18; Zech. 2-6; Jer. 3:11-15, 18; Apocrypha, 2 Esdras 13:40-47
14. See Ezra 1:1-11

1 And there was given me a reed like unto a rod: and the angel stood, saying, Rise, and measure the temple of God, and the altar, and them that worship therein.[15]

Concerning the outer court, why was John told not to measure it?

While all Saints shall have access to the outer court, only those who are judged worthy can go beyond the outer court into the temple proper.

What did the angel mean when he said, *"and the holy city shall they tread under foot forty and two months?"* It will be during this time that a vast army from the North will attempt to conquer Jerusalem and the nation of Israel. According to Joel, just the sight of this insurmountable force shall strike terror and panic within the hearts of the Jews. To help one visualize the destructive power of this army, Joel records that the land before them is like the Garden of Eden, while behind them lay a burning desolate wilderness. He then describes the assault tactics they shall use to conquer many cities.[16] This is important to know because those Saints who shall *not* measure up as being worthy to enter the temple shall be considered as *Gentiles* when the holy city is trodden underfoot and consequently shall forfeit any claim to divine protection.

2 But the court which is without the temple leave out, and measure it not; for it is given unto the Gentiles: and the holy city shall they tread under foot forty and two months.[17]

What wonder will God perform to facilitate an accepting heart in the children of Judah?

---

15. Rev. 11:1
16. See Joel 2:2-10
17. Rev. 11:2

When the temple is operationally ready, two individuals shall appear in Jerusalem. John simply refers to these people as the *two witnesses*. They shall prophesy, where Christ was crucified (Jerusalem),[18] for three and a half Biblical years (42 months) clothed in sackcloth.

As mentioned previously, Israel shall be given seven years to reconcile with Christ.[19] This seven-year period shall commence when the disciples of Christ dedicate their temple unto the Lord.

> 3 And I will give power unto my two witnesses, and they shall prophesy a thousand two hundred and threescore days, clothed in sackcloth.
> 4 These are the two olive trees, and the two candlesticks standing before the God of the earth.[20]

While these two prophets are prophesying in Jerusalem, how will they stave off a clandestine effort to silence them?

As Israel is under siege, these two prophets shall be given divine power to smite the earth with various plagues until they have finished testifying of Christ. Eventually, the Lord shall cause this army to be driven back to the North from whence they came,[21] however, only one sixth of the original force shall still be alive.[22] Thus, these two witnesses shall be the instruments by which this northern army shall be defeated in their bid to capture the nation of Israel. Interestingly, instead of receiving the acclamation they deserve, these two witnesses shall be hated and vilified for prophesying and testifying of Jesus Christ.

---

18. See Rev. 11:8
19. See Dan. 9:27
20. Rev. 11:3, 4

21. See Joel 2:20
22. See Ezek. 39:2

> *5 And if any man will hurt them, fire proceedeth out of their mouth, and devoureth their enemies: and if any man will hurt them, he must in this manner be killed.*
> *6 These have power to shut heaven, that it rain not in the days of their prophecy: and have power over waters to turn them to blood, and to smite the earth with all plagues, as often as they will.[23]*

What will happen to these two witnesses?

Eventually, the beast, who ascends out of the bottomless pit, will kill them, and their bodies shall lie in the streets of Jerusalem for three and a half days while their enemies send gifts one to another to celebrate their demise.

> *7 And when they shall have finished their testimony, the beast that ascendeth out of the bottomless pit shall make war against them, and shall overcome them, and kill them.*
> *8 And their dead bodies shall lie in the street of the great city, which spiritually is called Sodom and Egypt, where also our Lord was crucified.*
> *9 And they of the people and kindreds and tongues and nations shall see their dead bodies three days and an half, and shall not suffer their dead bodies to be put in graves.*
> *10 And they that dwell upon the earth shall rejoice over them, and make merry, and shall send gifts one to another; because these two prophets tormented them that dwelt on the earth.[24]*

As the dead bodies of the two witnesses lie in the streets of Jerusalem, what will happen next?

According to Daniel, the temple shall be polluted as the abomination that maketh desolate is set up. Moreover, the disciples of

---

23. Rev. 11:5, 6
24. Rev. 11:7-10

Christ who shall sacrifice their time and effort to perform this temple work shall be shorn of their duties. Then the sacred holy place shall be plundered, and the hallowed ordinances blasphemed as the truth is twisted and cast to the ground. This is the abomination of desolation, spoken of by Daniel the prophet.

> *31 And arms shall stand on his part, and they shall pollute the sanctuary of strength, and shall take away the daily sacrifice, and they shall place the abomination that maketh desolate.*[25]
>
> *11 Yea, he magnified himself even to the prince of the host, and by him the daily sacrifice was taken away, and the place of his sanctuary was cast down.*
>
> *12 And an host was given him against the daily sacrifice by reason of trangression, and it cast down the truth to the ground; and it practised, and prospered.*[26]

After the two witnesses are killed, what will happen to their bodies?

Following this event, the bodies shall be taken up to heaven while their enemies witness their resurrection with great fear and trepidation.

> *11 And after three days and an half the Spirit of life from God entered into them, and they stood upon their feet; and great fear fell upon them which saw them.*
>
> *12 And they heard a great voice from heaven saying unto them, Come up hither. And they ascended up to heaven in a cloud; and their enemies beheld them.*[27]

---

25. Dan. 11:31
26. Dan. 8:11, 12
27. Rev. 11:11, 12

When this abomination of desolation takes place, what prophecy will be fulfilled?

It is a prophecy, recorded by Matthew, that was originally given to warn Judah of their pending destruction. The Jews did not heed this warning and the Roman army destroyed Jerusalem, along with their holy temple in 70 A.D.

It should be noted, however, that this prophecy is a type and shadow, and is intended to warn Judah of what to expect when the House of the Lord is desecrated and the *abomination that maketh desolate* is revealed.[28]

Though much destruction will occur, the Saints shall have no need to fear. They shall be under God's protection, much as when the early Christian Saints were protected from the approaching Roman army during their evacuation to the town of Pella in 70 A.D. In like manner, the followers of Christ will be led to their *holy place* before the great tribulation shall occur.

> *15 When ye therefore shall see the abomination of desolation, spoken of by Daniel the prophet, stand in the holy place, (whoso readeth, let him understand:)*
> *16 Then let them which be in Judea flee into the mountains:*
> *17 Let them which is on the housetop not come down to take any thing out of his house:*
> *18 Neither let him which is in the field return back to take his clothes.*
> *19 And woe unto them that are with child, and to them that give suck in those days!*
> *20 But pray ye that your fight be not in the winter, neither on the sabbath day:*
> *21 For then shall be great tribulation, such as was not since the beginning of the world to this time, no, nor ever shall be.*

---

28. 2 Thes. 2:4

22 And except those days should be shortened, there should no flesh be saved: but for the elect's sake those days shall be shortened.[29]

What devastating event is about to happen, and how will it help convince a portion of Israel to accept the true and everlasting gospel?

Jerusalem shall experience a great earthquake. This quake will destroy one tenth of the city, and slay seven thousand men. Moreover, it will be the instrument that shall turn a number of Jews to Christ. The individuals who will give glory to God shall be those who finally comprehend why the wrath of God is kindled against them.

In this case, the term *"seven thousand"* is not to be taken literally, since the number seven indicates perfection, the number of deaths shall be enough to bring about a change of heart for those who sincerely want to believe.

It is also important to understand that when the destructive power of God's wrath falls upon, both the enemies of Israel and Israel herself, it shall provide the opportunity whereby a fourth Jewish temple can be constructed upon the holy temple mount. Thus, this quake delineates that period when the second woe is past and the third woe begins.

13 And the same hour was there a great earthquake, and the tenth part of the city fell, and in the earthquake were slain of men seven thousand: and the remnant were affrighted, and gave glory to the God of heaven.
14 The second woe is past; and, behold, the third woe cometh quickly.[30]

---

29. Matt. 24:15-22
30. Rev. 11:13, 14

Is this the same earthquake that is mentioned in chapter 6, concerning the sixth seal?

The answer is yes. As previously mentioned, when John opened the sixth seal he observed a great earthquake, then the sun turned black, and the moon became as blood. Following this, the stars appeared to fall from the sky, then the heaven *departed*, as a scroll when it is rolled together. The power of this earthquake is so strong that it caused every mountain and island to be moved out of its place. Such fear arose in the hearts of men that kings, great men, rich men, chief captains, mighty men, bonds men, and free men all tried to hide in the dens and rocks of the mountains in hopes that they could find protection from the wrath of the Lamb (Jesus Christ). *For the great day of his wrath is come and who will be able to stand.*[31] But why is this destruction so pervasive?

In chapter 7, as previously discussed, John saw an angel declaring to four other angels (who had the power to unleash the divine forces of nature) to not hurt the earth until a global missionary effort, to locate and secure all individuals who want to come unto Christ, had been completed. To accomplish this, the Savior initially sent out millions of missionaries to prepare the wheat for the harvest, then, as a final effort, He dispatched another *144,000* to comb the corners of the fields. Additionally, two special witnesses were sent to Israel, only to receive a martyr's reward. Thus fulfilling the divine requirement which states: *"At the mouth of two witnesses, or three witnesses, shall he that is worthy of death be put to death; but at the mouth of one witness he shall not be put to death."*[32] The demise of these two witnesses marks the moment when judgment cometh and the Lord begins to preach His own testimony of wrath and destruction upon the wicked and proud of this world.

---

31. Rev. 6:17
32. Deut. 17:6

Is this destruction the same event John witnessed regarding the seven thunders, but was forbidden to write about?

Again, the answer is yes. As discussed before in chapter 10, John saw the mighty angel (Michael) come down from heaven. He cried with a loud voice, and in response the seven thunders uttered their voices. Then Michael (after making a solemn pledge to God) declared that there should be time no longer. Since John was forbidden to write about this event, one is left to wonder what had happened?

What John saw, was Michael authorizing the seven thunders to carry out their assigned task of initiating this wrath, because the moment to complete a global missionary operation had expired. It's now time for the seventh angel to sound his trump so the Lord can finish the remainder of His work that must be accomplished before the Second Coming can occur. This is why John was told, *"The second woe is past; and, behold, the third woe cometh quickly."*[33]

---

33. Rev. 11:14

12

The Role of Satan

Before the final harvest begins, an angel presents John with another historical flashback. This knowledge helps John understand the role Satan plays in God's overall plan of salvation and how the adversary shall assist in bringing to fruition the main harvest of man.

This vision chronicles the efforts of Satan to prevent the Church of Jesus Christ from bringing forth the Kingdom of Heaven upon the earth, and explains how this battle began in heaven before spreading to this world. The angel recounts Satan's success in (repeatedly) thwarting God's plan to establish His earthly kingdom. However, eventually, the Saints shall achieve victory by keeping the commandments of God and maintaining a testimony of Jesus Christ.

What did John see in heaven?

John now beholds a woman, and upon her head is a crown of twelve stars. This woman represents the Church of Jesus Christ, as signified by the twelve stars. These stars denote the twelve apostles who are the foundation of the Church.[1] The woman is also pregnant with child and is ready to deliver. The child represents the Kingdom of Heaven, which is God's earthly system of government. *"And he said unto them. When ye pray, say, Our Father which art in heaven, Hallowed be thy name. Thy kingdom come. Thy will be done, as in heaven, so in earth."*[2]

> *1 And there appeared a great wonder in heaven; a woman clothed with the sun, and the moon under her feet, and upon her head a crown of twelve stars:*
> *2 And she being with child cried, travailing in birth, and pained to be delivered.*[3]

Who was the red dragon?

In the heavenly vision, John observes a red dragon having seven heads and ten horns, with seven crowns upon the heads. The red dragon is Satan.[4] The identification of the seven heads, ten horns, and seven crowns upon their heads shall be given later in chapter 13.

> *3 And there appeared another wonder in heaven; and behold a great red dragon, having seven heads and ten horns, and seven crowns upon his heads.*[5]

Who are the stars of heaven?

The stars of heaven are the spirit children of God. What John sees is Satan being cast out of heaven to earth thereby drawing

1. See Eph. 2:19-21; 4:11; 1 Cor. 12:28; Rev. 21:14   4. See Rev. 12:9
2. Luke 11:2   5. Rev. 12:3
3. Rev. 12:1, 2

a third part of the spirit children of God along with him.[6] Satan now stands ready to devour the child as soon as it is born.

> *4 And his tail drew the third part of the stars of heaven, and did cast them to the earth: and the dragon stood before the woman which was ready to be delivered, for to devour her child as soon as it was born.*[7]

What happened to the man child?

As previously explained, the man child represents the Kingdom of Heaven, which is God's earthly system of government. Eventually, the child is caught up unto God. This occurred when Jesus Christ and His apostles were martyred, and the keys of the Kingdom of Heaven were taken from the earth.

> *5 And she brought forth a man child, who was to rule all nations with a rod of iron: and her child was caught up unto God, and to his throne.*[8]

Why did the woman flee into the wilderness?

The angel explains to John that the woman (Church) shall flee into the wilderness (place of protection) until the time is right when she can be restored to the world.[9] According to the Greek Dictionary of the New Testament the word *days*, as shown below, can also be interpreted as *years*.[10]

> *6 And the woman fled into the wilderness, where she hath a place prepared of God, that they should feed her there a thousand two hundred and threescore days.*[11]

---

6. Rev. 12:7, 8
7. Rev. 12:4
8. Rev. 12:5
9. See Rev. 12:13-14

10. Strong's Concordance of the Bible, Greek Dictionary of the New Testament, Page 35, Reference: 2250
11. Rev. 12:6

Why were Satan and his followers cast out of heaven?

According to Isaiah, in pre-mortal life, Satan (Lucifer) tried to usurp the authority of God.[12] Because of this, there was a war in heaven. Michael and his angels fought against Satan and his angels. Michael won that battle and the accuser of the brethren (Satan) and his angels were cast onto the earth.

Thus, Satan has an army of spirits to help him carry out his goals. This is why the angel added the ominous warning: *"Woe to the inhabiters of the earth... for the devil is come down unto you, having great wrath, because he knoweth that he hath but a short time."*

> *7 And there was war in heaven: Michael and his angels fought against the dragon; and the dragon fought and his angels,*
> *8 And prevailed not; neither was their place found any more in heaven.*
> *9 And the great dragon was cast out, that old serpent, called the Devil, and Satan, which deceiveth the whole world: he was cast out into the earth, and his angels were cast out with him.*
> *10 And I heard a loud voice saying in heaven, Now is come salvation, and strength, and the kingdom of our God, and the power of his Christ: for the accuser of our brethren is cast down, which accused them before our God day and night.*
> *11 And they overcame him by the blood of the Lamb, and by the word of their testimony; and they loved not their lives unto the death.*
> *12 Therefore rejoice, ye heavens, and ye that dwell in them. Woe to the inhabiters of the earth and of the sea! for the devil is come down unto you, having great wrath, because he knoweth that he hath but a short time."*[13]

---

12. See Isa. 14:12-15
13. Rev. 12:7-12

What will happen after the Church is restored from the wilderness?

It was made known to John that after the Church is restored from the wilderness, Satan shall *again* begin to persecute the Saints by casting doubt and derision upon the validity of the Church, however, he shall not succeed.

> *13 And when the dragon saw that he was cast unto the earth, he persecuted the woman which brought forth the man child.*
>
> *14 And to the woman were given two wings of a great eagle, that she might fly into the wilderness, into her place, where she is nourished for a time, and times, and half a time, from the face of the serpent.*
>
> *15 And the serpent cast out of his mouth water as a flood after the woman, that he might cause her to be carried away of the flood.*
>
> *16 And the earth helped the woman, and the earth opened her mouth, and swallowed up the flood which the dragon cast out of his mouth.*
>
> *17 And the dragon was wroth with the woman, and went to make war with the remnant of her seed, which keep the commandments of God, and have the testimony of Jesus Christ.*[14]

14. Rev.12:13-17

13

The Role of the Beast & the False Prophet

U pon learning of what role the adversary shall play during last days, John is ready to receive more knowledge concerning Satan's rulers. The angel wants him to know how these dictators shall affect humanity between the sounding of the seventh trumpet and the final coming of the Son of God. This vision is to inform John that, in the last days, Satan shall prepare a protégé (referred to as the beast) to try and destroy God's plan to save mankind from spiritual death. This powerful ruler shall make his appearance *after* the initial wrath of God has been dispensed upon the earth. He shall be given control over all nations and the world shall worship him. He shall pretend to be religious and shall achieve success in warring against the Saints, until the arrival of the Second Coming.

John also sees a second beast; this individual shall assist the first beast in carrying out his objectives. This person shall exercise all the power of the first beast and shall perform great miracles. This second beast shall cause all to worship the first beast by controlling a persons ability to buy and sell, and shall also achieve great success, until the Lord intervenes.

What did John witness concerning the beast, seven heads, ten horns, and ten crowns?

He sees a beast rise up out of the sea having seven heads, ten horns with ten crowns, and written upon each head is the word *blasphemy*.

According to the information given to John in chapter 17, the sea represents peoples, multitudes, nations and tongues.[1] Therefore, the beast itself is a kingdom or nation consisting of many people that shall be raised up in the last days.[2]

The seven heads represent seven kings or rulers, who (through their actions) have elevated the kingdom of Satan in terms of power, prestige, and prominence. Six of these rulers are now dead; the seventh is the one who shall be in power over this nation during the last days,[3] and *when the nation and ruler act as one, it is the ruler who shall carry the title of beast.*[4]

The ten horns represent ten kingdoms. And the ten crowns are ten kings who shall reign over these kingdoms. These individuals have received no kingdom as yet, but shall receive power (as kings) for one hour (42 months) with the beast.[5]

The name blasphemy, as seen written upon their heads, symbolizes how they blaspheme God the Father and Jesus Christ by standing in opposition to their goal of bringing to pass the immortality and eternal life of all mankind.

> *1 And I stood upon the sand of the sea, and saw a beast rise up out of the sea, having seven heads and ten horns, and upon his horns ten crowns, and upon his heads the name of blasphemy.*[6]

---

1. Rev. 17:15   5. See Rev.17:12; 13:4-7
2. See Dan. 7:3, 23   6. Rev. 13:1
3. Rev. 17:10
4. See Rev. 13:3-5

How is the beast (nation) like a leopard, bear, and lion?

As mentioned previously, normally the beast is a nation. John is told that this nation has the capability to destroy with the ferocity of a leopard, tear apart as a bear, and like a lion chew to pieces any nation that dares to hinder its progress. This is important, because generally, while a single powerful nation is compared only to one type of wild animal, this nation is compared to three.[7]

Thus, this nation has the ability to destroy with great precision and awesome power. Where will it get this great power? John learns that Satan shall give this nation its power and authority.

> *2 And the beast which I saw was like unto a leopard, and his feet were as the feet of a bear, and his mouth as the mouth of a lion: and the dragon gave him his power, and his seat, and great authority.[8]*

What will happen to the seventh beast (ruler)?

After he assumes control over the nation that is like a leopard, bear, and lion (at some point during this time) he will receive what appears to be a mortal wound; however, this deadly wound shall be healed.

> *3 And I saw one of his heads as it were wounded to death; and his deadly wound was healed: and all the world wondered after the beast.[9]*

From where will the seventh beast receive his power?

---

7. See Dan 7:7
8. Rev. 13:2
9. Rev. 13:3

He will receive his power from Satan. Many shall say no one is like this ruler, who can win against him? Thus, most of the world shall unknowingly worship Satan because he is the hidden force behind the beast.

> 4 And they worshipped the dragon which gave power unto the beast: and they worshipped the beast, saying, Who is like unto the beast? who is able to make war with him?[10]

What other traits will this seventh beast possess?

This beast shall have the ability to make great speeches. Though he shall appear to be religious, his actions shall blaspheme the teachings of Christ. This world leader shall be in power before the angel sounds the seventh trumpet, and shall be given authority to remain in power for another 42 months.

> 5 And there was given unto him a mouth speaking great things and blasphemies; and power was given unto him to continue forty and two months.[11]

How will this beast blaspheme God?

Though he shall initially pretend to be religious, he shall eventually blaspheme the name of God, and all the Saints who dwell in heaven by desecrating their sacred tabernacle. This is the same person who, as prophesied by Paul, shall defile the temple that shall be built in Jerusalem.[12]

> 6 And he opened his mouth in blasphemy against God, to blaspheme his name, and his tabernacle, and them that dwell in heaven.[13]

---

10. Rev. 13:4   13. Rev. 13:6
11. Rev. 13:5
12. 2 Thes. 2:4

Why will the Lord allow this beast to make war with the Saints?

He will allow this because it shall facilitate His overall plan. That reason will be discussed in the next chapter.

> *7 And it was given unto him to make war with the saints, and to overcome them: and power was given him over all kindreds, and tongues, and nations.*[14]

From the clues provided, what can we surmise about this beast?

The clues indicate that a ruler shall rise to power over that great nation that has the ability to destroy like a leopard, bear, and lion. During the course of his reign, he shall receive what appears to be a mortal wound. However, this wound shall heal so that he shall suffer no harm. He is a powerful speaker; however, he shall blaspheme or disrespect the laws of God.

By using these clues the following picture begins to emerge. In the last days, a person with the ability to sway multitudes with his powerful oratory shall be elected as the leader of a super-power nation. He shall then become the seventh beast. He shall disrespect the laws of God, and during his term in office shall suffer what appears to be a mortal blow to his political career, however, he shall eventually recover. After his term of office expires, he shall rise to a position of world leader.

It should be noted that some scholars believe that an *actual* sword shall cause the wound.[15] This interpretation is too constricting. In the scriptures, *sword* can be interpreted as *word* or *truth*.[16]

---

14. Rev. 13:7
15. See Rev. 13:3, 14
16. See Heb. 4:12; Psalms 33:4, 117:2

What will be the penalty for those who worship this beast?

All individuals who end up worshipping this leader shall *not* have their names written in the book of life. If a person does not have his name in the book of life, he (or she) shall not be able to obtain eternal life.[17]

> 8 And all that dwell upon the earth shall worship him, whose names are not written in the book of life of the Lamb slain from the foundation of the world.[18]

What is the interpretation of: "If any man have an ear, let him hear"?

The Lord said: *"And he that overcometh, and keepeth my works unto the end, to him will I give power over the nations: ...He that overcometh, the same shall be clothed in white raiment; and I will not blot out his name out of the book of life... He that hath an ear, let him hear what the Spirit saith unto the churches."*[19]

> 9 If any man have an ear, let him hear.[20]

What is the meaning of: "He that leadeth into captivity shall go into captivity, and he that killeth with the sword must be killed with the sword?"

In the last days, as the beast makes war with the Saints, numerous individuals shall be taken captive and killed for their beliefs in the gospel of Jesus Christ. As horrible as this may

---

17. Dan. 12:1, 2; Rev. 21:27   19. Rev. 2:26; 3:5, 6
18. Rev. 13:8   20. Rev. 13:9

be, the remaining Saints are cautioned to exercise patience and remember that those who are committing these atrocities shall meet a similar fate.

> *10 He that leadeth into captivity shall go into captivity: he that killeth with the sword must be killed with the sword. Here is the patience and the faith of the saints.*[21]

What do we need to know about the beast?

We need to be able to recognize the beast when he steps onto the world stage. These are some of the clues to his identity. This leader shall possess the following attributes:

- He shall rise to power in the last days.[22]
- He shall lead a great powerful nation.[23]
- He shall receive a deadly wound to the head which will heal.[24]
- The world shall worship him.[25]
- The world shall say no one is like him.[26]
- The world shall ask who can make war with him?[27]
- He shall be a great speaker.[28]
- He shall blaspheme God by pretending to be religious.[29]
- He shall blaspheme God by speaking in His name.[30]
- He shall blaspheme God by desecrating His tabernacle.[31]
- He shall blaspheme the Saints in heaven by ridiculing their beliefs.[32]
- He shall possess the power to successfully war against the Saints.[33]

---

21. Rev. 13:10
22. See Rev. 17:10
23. See Rev. 13:2-4
24. See Rev. 13:3
25. See Rev. 13:4, 8
26. See Rev. 13:4
27. See Rev. 13:4
28. See Rev. 13:5
29. See Rev. 13:5
30. See Rev. 13:6
31. See Rev. 13:6
32. See Rev. 13:6
33. See Rev. 13:7

- He shall be given power over all nations.[34]
- He shall be the seventh in a succession of seven world leaders, of which six are already dead.[35]

Who is the second beast?

John sees another beast come up out of the earth. This beast has two horns, is like a lamb, and speaks like a dragon. The symbolism used to describe this beast is unique; nevertheless, it can be deciphered.

Long ago, when King David committed adultery with Bathsheba she became pregnant. To keep the world from discovering what really happened, David had Bathsheba's husband killed in battle. Later, the prophet Nathan chastised David and compared him to a thief who stole another person's lamb. Thus, Nathan compared the woman, Bathsheba to a lamb.[36]

Another clue to the identity of this person is this, whereas the first beast (nation) comes up out of the sea, this second beast comes up out of the earth. Indicating that the same elements that make up the earth can be found in the body of this beast.[37] Concerning the two horns, in Biblical terminology a horn signifies a source of power.[38] The two horns indicate two sources of power. The term, speaks as a dragon shows, that while this beast is portrayed as innocent, and defenseless, the speech pattern, used by this person, is closer to the type of emotional diatribe Satan would use. This beast is also known as the false prophet.[39]

With this information another picture begins to materialize, this person is a *woman*, who has a tendency, if necessary, to use strong emotional language to get what she wants. (Supporting evidence for this conclusion is presented later in this chapter.)

---

34. See Rev. 13:7
35. See Rev. 17:10
36. See 2 Sam. 12:1-10
37. See Gen. 3:19
38. See Dan. 8:7
39. See Rev. 16:13

Concerning the two sources of power, one source shall come from her relationship with this world leader, and the second source stems from an important position, which she shall hold. This beast is also known as the false prophet, because she believes she can foretell the future. She tries to communicate with the dead for inspiration and guidance; however, any effort to predict the future from this tenuous source will result in catastrophic failure. One question does remain: *Why would John use the term "he" when referring to this beast?* It could be that the Lord did not want John to know the gender of the beast. Thus, when John saw the beast, he simple assumed it was a *"he."*

> *11 And I beheld another beast coming up out of the earth; and he had two horns like a lamb, and he spake as a dragon.*[40]

How could this false prophet exercise all the power of the first beast?

She can exercise all the power of the first beast because she holds the same position once held by him. As the leader of a super power nation, she can exercise her influence to support his agenda of world domination, and she shall do everything possible to promote the veneration of the first beast because it shall help satisfy her own desire for wealth, power, and adulation.

> *12 And he exerciseth all the power of the first beast before him, and causeth the earth and them which dwell therein to worship the first beast, whose deadly wound was healed.*[41]

How does the false prophet make fire come down from heaven?

---

40. Rev. 13:11
41. Rev. 13:12

As commander and chief of the nation's armed forces, she has the power to call down firepower from aircraft, ships, and missile batteries against any perceived enemy.

> *13 And he doeth great wonders, so that he maketh fire come down from heaven on the earth in the sight of men,*[42]

How does the false prophet deceive people by these miracles, and why would this person want the people of the earth to make an image to the first beast?

Because of her position as the president of a great nation, she is able to convince many who dwell on the earth that it would be in their best interest to make an "*image*" to the beast.

One of the definitions of the word "*image*" is "reflection." This "*image*" is something that reflects the goals of the beast and helps him obtain what he wants. The goal of the beast is to achieve all power, strength, and glory. He wants total control and dominion over every person on earth. To achieve this total control he must have total loyalty and commitment of all concerned. Just as the golden "*image*" of Nebuchadnezzar was designed to determine who was loyal to the king;[43] the beast needs an "*image*" that can help him obtain the allegiance he so desperately wants. In this particular case, the "*image*" is a sophisticated identification system, which shall be used to determine who is certified to buy and sell. However, since this "*image*" represents the beast, to obtain certification, one must *first* give him their pledge of allegiance.

Because of her position, the false prophet shall have the power to give life to the development and implementation of this system. This "*image*" shall be revered, because it shall give

---

42. Rev. 13:13
43. See Dan. 3:1, 7

a person, not only the power to buy and sell, but the opportunity to stay alive. Since this identification system can determine the loyalty of a person (and has the capability to communicate this information to others) it shall possess the capacity to cause the death of anyone who shall not support the beast.

> *14 And deceiveth them that dwell on the earth by the means of those miracles which he had power to do in the sight of the beast; saying to them that dwell on the earth, that they should make an image to the beast, which had the wound by a sword, and did live.*
>
> *15 And he had power to give life unto the image of the beast, that the image of the beast should both speak, and cause that as many as would not worship the image of the beast should be killed.*[44]

What is the mark of the beast?

The mark is the code required by the beast to access the sophisticated identification system. This mark shall have the name of the beast, or the number of his name imbedded within the code. Either an eye or hand scanner shall be used to read the mark.

> *16 And he causeth all, both small and great, rich and poor, free and bond, to receive a mark in their right hand, or in their foreheads:*
>
> *17 And that no man might buy or sell, save he that had the mark, or the name of the beast, or the number of his name.*[45]

---

44. Rev. 13:14, 15
45. Rev. 13:16, 17

What is the meaning of the number six hundred threescore and six?

Throughout history society has exhibited a tendency to label certain individuals with various numbers. For example, it is not unusual for our current generation of young men to assign a number of *1* thru *10* to indicate the attractiveness of a young woman, with *1* being the least appealing to *10* being the ultimate beauty. The ancient Hebrews also used numbers to rank the attributes of certain individuals. For example, the number *7* was used to indicate total perfection. The ancient Hebrews also used the number *6* to indicate a quality that is very good, but falls short of perfection. Thus, if a man possessed the skills of a great orator, a person of ancient Hebrew origin might refer to this individual as a *6* in public speaking ability.

However, what about the beast? An angel told the prophet John that the number of the beast was six hundred threescore and six, or *666*. This would indicate that the beast would be gifted with three important assets, but what are they? Daniel provided the answer when he informed Nebuchadnezzar, *"Thou, O king, art a king of kings: for the God of heaven hath given thee a kingdom, power, and strength, and glory."*[46] Consequently, the numbers *666* indicate the grade of the three major gifts. The first *6* represent's the enormous *power* the beast would enjoy. The second *6* references the immense *strength* the beast would exhibit. And the third *6* is used to identify the vast *glory* that the beast will achieve.

But how can this information, concerning Nebuchadnezzar, be applicable to the beast of Revelation? To find out, one must go to the Book of Daniel and review an incident that happened to King Nebuchadnezzar during the second year of his reign.

---

46. Dan. 2:37

One night the king experienced a dream. The next morning he could not remember the dream, except that it troubled him very deeply. To resolve this dilemma he went to his magicians, astrologers, sorcerers, and Chaldeans for the answer. Since Nebuchadnezzar could not recall the dream, his wise men responded by informing the king they could not interpret the dream unless he told them what the dream was all about. Becoming increasingly frustrated, Nebuchadnezzar threatened his wise men with their lives unless they provided the right answer. Concluding that no man living on the earth could answer such a request, the men frantically began searching for a solution.

Upon learning that his life was also in danger, Daniel prayed to know the specifics of the king's dream. Once he had received an answer, Daniel, after being allowed to approach the king, informed Nebuchadnezzar that the God of Heaven had made known to him the dream and the interpretation thereof.

"Thou, O king, sawest, and behold a great image, This great image, whose brightness was excellent, stood before thee; and the form thereof was terrible. This image's head was of fine gold, his breast and his arms of silver, his belly and his thighs of brass, His legs of iron, his feet part of iron and part of clay. Thou sawest till that a stone was cut without hands, which smote the image upon his feet that were of iron and clay, and brake them to pieces. Then was the iron, the clay, the brass, the silver, and the gold, broken to pieces together, and became like the chaff of the summer threshingfloors; and the wind carried them away, that no place was found for them: and the stone that smote the image became a great mountain, and filled the whole earth."[47]

The important points to remember about this dream are these: What Nebuchadnezzar saw was a great and frightening apparition. The image, standing before him, manifested an extremely bright light and appeared in the form of a man, as represented by the head,

---

47. Dan. 2:31-35

breast, arms, belly, thighs, legs and feet. As the dream progressed, a stone rolled forth and struck the image on the feet, thus causing it to crumble so completely that it disappeared forever. Next, the stone began growing until it covered the entire earth.

After explaining to Nebuchadnezzar the specifics concerning his dream, Daniel then preceded to give the interpretation:

"This is the dream; and we will tell the interpretation thereof before the king. Thou, O king, art a king of kings: for the God of heaven hath given thee a kingdom, power, and strength, and glory. And wheresoever the children of men dwell, the beasts of the field and the fowls of the heaven hath he given into thine hand, and hath made thee ruler over them all. Thou art this head of gold. And after thee shall arise another kingdom inferior to thee, and another third kingdom of brass, which shall bear rule over all the earth. And the fourth kingdom shall be strong as iron: forasmuch as iron breaketh in pieces and subdueth all things: and as iron that breaketh all these, shall it break in pieces and bruise. And whereas thou sawest the feet and toes, part of potters' clay, and part of iron, the kingdom shall be divided; but there shall be in it of the strength of the iron, forasmuch as thou sawest the iron mixed with miry clay. And as the toes of the feet were part of iron, and part of clay, so the kingdom shall be partly strong, and partly broken. And whereas thou sawest iron mixed with miry clay, they shall mingle themselves with the seed of men: but they shall not cleave one to another, even as iron is not mixed with clay. And in the days of these kings shall the God of heaven set up a kingdom, which shall never be destroyed: and the kingdom shall not be left to other people, but it shall break in pieces and consume all these kingdoms, and it shall stand for ever. Forasmuch as thou sawest that the stone was cut out of the mountain without hands, and that it brake in pieces the iron, the brass, the clay, the silver, and the gold; the great God hath made known to the king what

shall come to pass hereafter: and the dream is certain, and the interpretation thereof sure."[48]

As outlined above, Daniel begins the conversation by informing the king that the God of Heaven has given Nebuchadnezzar a kingdom of power, strength, and glory. Daniel then interprets his dream as follows: The brightness of the image, indicates prestige or glory. The head, breast, arms, belly, thighs, legs, and feet all refer to diverse kingdoms, ruled by a king or sovereign ruler. The different type of metal that represents each kingdom, is a reference to their power, wealth, or strength. Some kingdoms, associated with the feet and toes of the image, have clay mixed with iron, thus indicating seams of weakness that permeate their empires.

The stone is the *Kingdom of God* that shall be established upon the earth in the last days. This *kingdom* begins to roll forth as a small stone, but shall grow in size, until it eventually collides into the feet of the image, thus causing the entire figure to collapse into total oblivion.

This dream, King Nebuchadnezzar witnessed, was a type and shadow of the beast that shall rise up in the last days to reign over the inhabitants' of the earth. This beast shall incorporate all the characteristics portrayed in the monarch's dream. He shall reign over a mighty kingdom and exude a forceful presence to all those who worship and oppose him. The gold, silver, and brass, all symbolize the enormous wealth he shall amass. The iron denotes his ability to conquer and subjugate his enemies. Ten kings shall put their country's resources behind him, as represented by the ten toes supporting the beast in Nebuchadnezzar's dream. However, at the time of the end, his kingdom shall also be destroyed along with all who support him.

How do we know that the image Nebuchadnezzar saw is a type and shadow of the beast as described by John in this

---

48. Dan. 2:36-45

chapter? When the angel informs John, concerning the support the ten kings will provide to the beast in the last days, the answer to this question becomes readily apparent:

"And the ten horns which thou sawest are ten kings, which have received no kingdom as yet; but receive power as kings one hour with the beast. These have one mind, and shall give their power and strength unto the beast. These shall make war with the Lamb, and the Lamb shall overcome them: for he is Lord of lords and King of kings: and they that are with him are called, and chosen, and faithful."[49]

In sum, as Nebuchadnezzar was given *power, strength,* and *glory* to reign over his kingdom (and since he, Nebuchadnezzar, represents the head of the image) the beast shall be given the same resources of *power, strength,* and *glory* to reign over the latter-day kingdoms of the world (note that the ten kings mentioned above, will also give their power and strength unto the beast); and the number *666* simply represents the frightening degree of resources the beast shall possess to wreak havoc upon his opponents.

Another example of a near perfect *(666)* fighting machine was Goliath, who carried a *600* shekel spear head, was *6* cubits and a span in height, and was protected by *6* pieces of equipment. He also was felled by a smooth stone (cut without hands) from a brook of water.[50]

It should be noted, however, that as formidable as the beast shall become, one should never forget that the number *666* is still just the number of a man, and cannot compete with a God in heaven who is omnipotent, omnipresent, and omniscient. That is why the stone *(Kingdom of God)* shall roll forth and completely destroy the kingdom of the beast. Those individuals who, while living on the earth during this time, must make the decision concerning which kingdom they should join, would do

---

49. Rev. 17:12-14
50. 1 Sam. 17:4-7, 40, 49

well to seriously consider the words of Joshua, *"...but as for me and my house, we will serve the LORD."*[51]

> *18 Here is wisdom. Let him that hath understanding count the number of the beast: for it is the number of a man; and his number is Six hundred threescore and six.*[52]

At the beginning of the discussion, concerning who is the second beast? It was mentioned that this person is a woman. Is there any evidence to support this conclusion?

In chapter 3, it was revealed that a third Jezebel shall arise during the last days and that this woman shall possess many of the same traits already exhibited by the first two Jezebels.

Thus to find out if this woman could be the second beast or false prophet of the last days, let us compare the information outlined in chapter 3, concerning the first two Jezebels with the false prophet. As Jezebel possessed two sources of power (as the daughter of a monarch and wife to the king of Israel); in like manner, the false prophet shall have two sources of power (as president of a great nation and spouse to the ruler of the world). As Jezebel had the cunning ability to talk her cohorts into committing murder for land; in like manner, the false prophet shall use her satanic speaking ability to convince her followers to massacre the Saints who will refuse to take on the mark of the beast. As Jezebel was able to exercise all the power of King Ahab by being his intimate confidant; in like manner, the false prophet shall exercise all the power of the first beast by being his closest personal advisor. As Jezebel induced her subjects to make an image to Baal; in like manner, the false prophet shall have her followers make an image to the first beast. As Jezebel

---

51. Josh. 24:15
52. Rev. 13:18

caused many of the Lord's prophets (who would not worship the image to Baal) to be put to death; in like manner, the false prophet shall cause many (who will not worship the image of the first beast) to be put to death. As Jezebel used her prophetic standing to seduce and destroy the Saints in Thyatira; in like manner, the false prophet shall use her prophetic reputation to seduce and devastate the Saints of the last days.

In sum, as Jezebel was a woman, it is apparent that the second beast, or false prophet is a woman – a woman - who shall be known as the third Jezebel of the Book of Revelation.

What do we need to know about the false prophet?

We need to be able to identify this person so we shall know when the false prophet arrives. Luke says that we can tell whether a person is good or evil by the fruit they bring forth.[53] Therefore, this is how we shall be able to recognize this individual:

- She shall have the outward appearance of a lamb.[54]
- She shall come up out of the earth.[55]
- She shall have two horns.[56]
- She shall speak as a dragon.[57]
- She shall exercise all the power of the first beast.[58]
- She shall cause all to worship the first beast.[59]
- She shall make fire come down from heaven.[60]
- She shall deceive all by means of miracles.[61]
- She shall have all make an *image* to the beast.[62]
- She shall give life to the *image* of the beast.[63]
- She shall cause the *image* of the beast to speak.[64]

---

53. See Luke 6:43, 44
54. Rev. 13:11
55. Rev. 13:11
56. Rev. 13:11
57. Rev. 13:11
58. Rev. 13:12
59. Rev. 13:12
60. Rev. 13:13
61. Rev. 13:14
62. Rev. 13:14
63. Rev. 13:15
64. Rev. 13:15

- She shall cause all who do not worship the *image* to be put to death.[65]

- She shall cause all to receive a mark, and decree that no man may buy or sell unless they have this mark.[66]

- She shall have the propensity to commune with the spirit world in order to receive guidance and direction, and thus will be known as the false prophet.[67]

---

65. Rev. 13:15
66. Rev. 13:16, 17
67. Rev. 16:13, 14

14

The Seventh Trumpet– the Harvest Begins

After witnessing the tribulation caused by the wrath of God, in the form of a great earthquake, John now has a greater understanding concerning what role the beast and the false prophet shall play during end-time events and is ready for the final reel of the big picture to begin. He sees the *144,000* servants of God, which were redeemed from the earth, and is told that these are they who were resurrected from among men, being the first fruits unto God and the Lamb. He also hears a loud voice saying, that it's time for the judgment to begin by rewarding the elect who have obeyed the commandments of God.

Another angel announces the fall of a great Babylonian city. A third angel forewarns the Saints that the time has arrived for them to reject any thought (even at the peril of their own lives) of taking on the mark of the beast. Then, the Son of Man reaps His righteous followers from the earth, and another angel gathers the wicked from Babylon to be cast into the winepress of the wrath of God.

When the seventh angel sounds, what will happen?

John sees twenty-four elders conversing in heaven. They announce that the time has arrived for the kingdoms of this world to become the Kingdoms of Jesus Christ. In other words, the time has arrived for Him to take control of earthly events. This is necessary so He can accomplish all that needs to be done to prepare the way before He can come forth victoriously on a white horse with great power and glory.

> 15 And the seventh angel sounded; and there were great voices in heaven, saying, The kingdoms of this world are become the kingdoms of our Lord, and of his Christ; and he shall reign for ever and ever.
> 16 And the four and twenty elders, which sat before God on their seats, fell upon their faces, and worshipped God,
> 17 Saying, We give thee thanks, O Lord God Almighty, which art, and wast, and art to come; because thou hast taken to thee thy great power, and hast reigned.[1]

What would be one of the first things the Lord would do as He begins His reign?

The Lord's first order of business is to judge the dead and reward His servants the prophets and the Saints who reverenced His name. His second priority shall be to destroy those who are destroying the earth.

> 18 And the nations were angry, and thy wrath is come, and the time of the dead, that they should be judged, and that

---

1. Rev. 11:15-17

thou shouldest give reward unto thy servants the prophets,
and to the saints, and them that fear thy name, small and
great; and shouldest destroy them which destroy the earth.[2]

What interesting observation did John make during his viewing of God's heavenly realm?

He sees that the temple doors are open. He also observes the ominous signs of lightning, thundering, earthquake, and great hail that shall soon afflict the earth.

> *19 And the temple of God was opened in heaven, and*
> *there was seen in his temple the ark of his testament: and*
> *there were lightnings, and voices, and thunderings, and*
> *an earthquake, and great hail.*[3]

Who did John see standing on Mount Zion?

As John looks, he beholds the Savior on Mount Zion (in heaven) and with Him stand the *144,000*, who have the name of the Father written in their foreheads, and all the tribes of Israel (except Dan) are represented in this group. Having His name written in their foreheads means their calling and election is made sure, thus they are sealed up unto eternal life and exaltation.[4]

> *1 And I looked, and, lo, a Lamb stood on the mount Sion,*
> *and with him an hundred forty and four thousand, having*
> *his Father's name written in their foreheads.*[5]

What will be one of the first things the 144,000 will do when they arrive in heaven?

_____

2. Rev. 11:18
3. Rev. 11:19
4. 2 Peter 1:10
5. Rev. 14:1

After being redeemed from the earth, they shall worship Christ by singing a special song that only the *144,000* have earned the right to sing.

> *2 And I heard a voice from heaven, as the voice of many waters, and as the voice of a great thunder: and I heard the voice of harpers harping with their harps:*
> *3 And they sung as it were a new song before the throne, and before the four beasts, and the elders: and no man could learn that song but the hundred and forty and four thousand, which were redeemed from the earth.[6]*

Were there other qualities these first fruits of the resurrection possessed that helped them achieve the seal of God?

They honored the covenant of chastity, and in their mouth was found no guile, therefore they were without fault in the eyes of God.

> *4 These are they which were not defiled with women; for they are virgins. These are they which follow the Lamb whithersoever he goeth. These were redeemed from among men, being the firstfruits unto God and to the Lamb.*
> *5 And in their mouth was found no guile: for they are without fault before the throne of God.[7]*

If the 144,000 are resurrected at this time, how will this event begin?

The angel (who controls the administration of the everlasting gospel) declares with a loud voice that *"judgment is come,"*

---

6. Rev. 14:2, 3
7. Rev. 14:4, 5

implying, that the time has come to judge the dead, and give reward to the prophets and Saints.

> 6 And I saw another angel fly in the midst of heaven, having the everlasting gospel to preach unto them that dwell on the earth, and to every nation, and kindred, and tongue, and people,
> 7 Saying with a loud voice, Fear God, and give glory to him; for the hour of his judgment is come: and worship him that made heaven, and earth, and the sea, and the fountains of waters.[8]

When John looked into heaven he saw that the temple was open, why is this important to note?

An Angel gives John part of the answer by saying, when the seventh trumpet begins to sound, the *mystery* of God shall be finished.

> 7 But in the days of the voice of the seventh angel, when he shall begin to sound, the mystery of God should be finished, as he hath declared to his servants the prophets.[9]

Did God provide the answer to this mystery?

The *mystery*, Paul said, is that at the last trump, *the dead shall be raised and we shall be changed. For this mortal must put on immortality.* Therefore, the doors to the temple are *open* to welcome a very select group of individuals. These are they who are redeemed of God, and because of their loyalty and steadfastness in obeying His commandments are rewarded with the honor of becoming the first fruits of the Resurrection.

---

8. Rev. 14:6, 7
9. Rev. 10:7

51 Behold I shew you a mystery; We shall not all sleep, but we shall all be changed,

52 In a moment, in the twinkling of an eye, at the last trump: for the trumpet shall sound, and the dead shall be raised incorruptible, and we shall be changed.

53 For this corruptible must put on incorruption, and this mortal must put on immortality.

54 So when this corruptible shall have put on incorruption, and this mortal shall have put on immortality, then shall be brought to pass the saying that is written, Death is swallowed up in victory.[10]

What heavenly event must take place before the resurrection process can begin?

According to Matthew, after the tribulation of those days (the great earthquake mentioned in chapter 6) the sun shall be darkened, the moon shall not give her light, and the stars shall fall from heaven.

29 Immediately after the tribulation of those days shall the sun be darkened, and the moon shall not give her light, and the stars shall fall from heaven, and the powers of the heavens shall be shaken.[11]

What will happen next?

Then shall appear the sign of the Son of Man, Matthew recorded, and they shall see Him coming with great power and glory.

30 And then shall appear the sign of the Son of man in heaven: and then shall all the tribes of the earth mourn, and they shall see the Son of man coming in the clouds of heaven with power and great glory.[12]

---

10. 1 Cor. 15:51-54
11. Matt. 24:29
12. Matt. 24:30

What is this sign?

When the Son of Man (Jesus Christ) makes His appearance, the light seen in the heavens shall be the *light* emanating from the glory of the Son of Man Himself, therefore, this "*light*" is the *sign* of the coming of the Son of Man.

> 27 For as the lightning cometh out of the east, and shineth even unto the west; so shall also the coming of the Son of man be.[13]

How will this resurrection occur?

The Lord shall descend from heaven, the apostle Paul added, and *the dead who served Christ shall rise first*; then *those who are alive* shall be caught up to meet the Lord in the air.

> 16 For the Lord himself shall descend from heaven with a shout, with the voice of the archangel, and with the trump of God: and the dead in Christ shall rise first:
> 17 Then we which are alive and remain shall be caught up together with them in the clouds, to meet the Lord in the air: and so shall we ever be with the Lord.[14]

Who else besides the 144,000 will be resurrected?

Then, noted Matthew, the angels shall gather His elect from the four corners of the earth. The Hebrew harvest had three different stages. It began with the first fruits. The main harvest was next, then the gleaning. By using the word "*elect*" Matthew gives us the identity of those who are caught up. This resurrection of the *elect* is analogous to the harvesting of the *elite* Saints of God.

---

13. Matt. 24:27
14. 1 Thes. 4:16-17

These are the *elect* members of the Church of Jesus Christ who shall hear the words, *"Because thou hast kept the word of my patience, I also will keep thee from the hour of temptation, which shall come upon all the world, to try them that dwell upon the earth."*[15] These are *also* they who shall heed the words, *"Watch ye therefore, and pray always, that ye may be accounted worthy to escape all these things that shall come to pass, and to stand before the Son of man."*[16]

> *31 And he shall send his angels with a great sound of a trumpet, and they shall gather together his elect from the four winds, from one end of heaven to the other.*[17]

Will the entire world witness the actual resurrection?

While all of the world shall see the sign of the coming of the Son of Man, only the *elect* shall be able to see the actual resurrection process. This is because only they shall have the spiritual eyes necessary to discern their Lord, much like Stephen was the only one to see God as he was being stoned to death.[18] Only their missing presence shall offer any clue as to what has just occurred. Though the world shall witness a strange brilliant light transiting from east to west, they shall rationalize it as just a near miss from a passing celestial phenomenon.

As the hour of temptation, which shall come upon all the world, draws nigh, what will the Lord do to protect the remnant of His followers?

The Lord, knowing that perilous times will soon fall upon the world, shall ensure that places of refuge are available for the remainder of His Saints. One of these sanctuary cities shall

---

15. Rev. 3:10
16. Luke 21:36
17. Matt. 24:31

18. See Acts 7:55-60

be called Mount Zion, in the land of America. The Saints living in the last days will build this city, and it shall be a site, not just for His Saints, but also for all people of every nation who are looking for a place of peace and safety. The city of refuge for the Jews shall be located in Jerusalem, where their holy temple shall stand. *"And it shall come to pass, that whosoever shall call on the name of the LORD shall be delivered: for in mount Zion and in Jerusalem shall be deliverance, as the LORD hath said, and in the remnant whom the LORD shall call."*[19] Since these sites shall enjoy heavenly protection, the wicked will avoid any contact for fear of divine retribution.

At this point, John is informed that a great Babylonian city shall fall. This is unusual because this prediction is too soon to be associated with the Babylonian destruction that shall occur just prior to the Second Coming. So what city could it possibly be?

Unfortunately, it will be the city of New York, in the United States of America. In order to understand why New York, it is necessary to review some of the different ways God attempts to help His earthly children. One way is to choose a nation and make an agreement with that nation that will benefit both God and man. This agreement is called a covenant. In this covenant God agrees to provide prosperity, protection, productivity, and contentment. And, in turn, the chosen nation agrees to walk in His statutes and keep His commandments.

This can be beneficial to both parties in several ways. First, it can help God's children to be raised in a protected environment surrounded by righteous believers and equipped with all the tools available to achieve immortality and eternal life.

19: Joel 2:32

Secondly, the chosen nation can, not only help other nations by providing protection, financial and other assistance, but can stand as a beacon of hope for any nation who wants to follow its precepts and garner heavenly blessings for their own people.

A great example of how this process works is to examine what happened around 1380 B.C. to the children of God after they were saved from the oppression of Egypt. When Moses and his followers arrived at mount Sinai, God offered the following covenant: *"If ye walk in my statutes, and keep my commandants, and do them; Then I will give you rain in due season, and the land shall yield her increase. . . and ye shall eat your bread to the full, and dwell in your land safely, And I will give peace in the land, and ye shall lie down, and none shall make you afraid: . . . For I will. . . make you fruitful, and multiply you, and establish my covenant with you . . . And I will set my tabernacle among you: . . . And I will walk among you, and will be your God, and ye shall be my people."*[20]

The children of Israel accepted this covenant and lived for hundreds of years in peace and prosperity. However, as the centuries passed, Israel began to reject their God and turn from His teachings. Finally, about 721 B.C., after having been warned,[21] God allowed ten of the twelve tribes of Israel to be captured and exiled to Assyria.[22] Then (following another warning in 590 B.C.,)[23] Nebuchadnezzar was permitted to conquer Jerusalem and exile the remaining tribes.[24] This occurred about 587 B.C.

But does God still make covenants in this day and age? Following the discovery of the new world in 1492, many people (such as the Puritans) migrated here to escape the tyranny of Europe and to find a place where they could worship God according to the dictates of their own conscience. At the time, of the ten major kingdoms that comprised the continent of Europe, there were three nations (Spain, France, and England)

20: Leviticus 26:3-12
21: 2 Kings 17:5
22: 2 Kings 17:6-18
23: 2 Kings 24:1
24: 2 Kings 24:2-20

that were actively competing for the opportunity to rule this new world. However, that would never happen because God had other plans.

By the middle of the sixteenth century, thirteen colonies had formed along the eastern coast of the new world. During an attempt to remove the shackles of foreign rule, an ensuing war broke out, pitting one of the world's greatest land and sea military forces against a group of rag-tag citizen militia with little training and no sea capability whatsoever. Through divine assistance, this small band of soldiers defeated one of the greatest armies of the time. Thus as Spain, France, and England jockeyed for position to determine who would rule this new world a new nation emerged from the competition and called itself, The United States of America.

With the help from divine providence, these thirteen colonies were able to develop a Constitution, and on April, 30, 1789, in the city of New York, George Washington placed his hand on the Holy Bible, and uttered these words: *"I do solemnly swear that I will faithfully execute the office of the President of the United States, and will to the best of my ability, preserve, protect, and defend the Constitution of the United Sates."*[25]

Since George Washington considered the Constitution a divinely inspired document, it becomes a type of covenant. In other words, an agreement that implies: *If we, the citizens of The United States of America, will govern ourselves according to the Constitution of this land, God will bless us with prosperity, protection, productivity, and contentment.*[26]

However, over the years we have steadily departed from the basic principles of this great document by first, increasingly rejecting a loving God who gave us this land. And secondly, by allowing the politicians of this great nation to purposely manipulate the system of checks and balances (written into the

---

25: Article II, Section I of the Constitution of the United States
26: George Washington, October 1789, as quoted in Novak and Novak, Washington's God, New York: Basic Books, 2006, 144-145

Constitution) to allow our elected leaders to impose immoral behavior (by legislation or executive decree) upon its citizens and armed forces.

Some have claimed that rejecting God from our public activities is necessary to preserve the separation between church and state. It should be noted, however, that the Constitution was never meant to alienate us from God. It was written to bring us closer to God by guarantying freedom of worship for all creeds who wish to worship according to the dictates of their own conscience and also, to prevent the rise of any single government-sponsored faith from imposing its will upon the rest of society. By allowing those who do not believe in a divine creator to compel their will upon all whom sincerely believe (in the guise of separation of church and state) places us on the same path that ancient Israel followed as it abandoned its God until finally, God rejected Israel.

Thus, New York, a city that once exemplified the words: *"Give Me your tired, your poor, your huddled masses yearning to breathe free,"* (as expressed by the Statue of Liberty) is now leading the charge towards self destruction by allowing the wicked designs of the adversary to permeate the hearts of its citizens, and the rest of the world as well.

Therefore, it was no accident that on September 11, 2001, a loving God, attempting to provide a wake-up call to the inhabitants of New York and the rest of the world, allowed this city to be on the receiving end of a calamity that would mark the starting point, whereby over the period of many years, various disasters, in the form of earthquakes, tornadoes, fires, and war shall increasingly rage until a third part of the earth's trees shall be burned, along with all the green grass. It was also no accident that ground zero for this destruction would take place within a short walking distance from where George Washington first placed his hand on the Bible in 1789 A.D. and covenanted with the citizens of this country and with God to uphold the Constitution of The United States of American.

Sadly, pride and arrogance shall prohibit any acknowledgment for the need to repent, thus sealing the fate of a once majestic city that shall fail to heed the admonition given by the Lord: *"If my people, which are called by my name, shall humble themselves, and pray, and seek my face, and turn from their wicked ways; then will I hear from heaven, and will forgive their sin, and will heal their land."*[27]

> *8 And there followed another angel, saying, Babylon is fallen, is fallen, that great city, because she made all nations drink of the wine of the wrath of her fornication.*[28]

What will happen to those who join forces with the beast?

An angel says with a loud voice, if any man *worship* the beast and his image, and *receive* his mark in his forehead, or in his hand, the same shall drink of the wine of the wrath of God, which is poured out without measure.

> *9 And the third angel followed them, saying with a loud voice, If any man worship the beast and his image, and receive his mark in his forehead, or in his hand,*
> *10 The same shall drink of the wine of the wrath of God, which is poured out without mixture into the cup of his indignation; and he shall be tormented with fire and brimstone in the presence of the holy angels, and in the presence of the Lamb:*[29]

---

27. 2 Chron. 7:14
28. Rev. 14:8
29. Rev. 14:9, 10

When the time arrives to decide whether to take the mark of the beast, what will take place?

On earth, the false prophet shall have the identification system "*image*" ready for use. It is time to see who shall pledge their allegiance by taking the mark of the beast. The big decision must now be made. *Do I choose life by pledging allegiance to the beast and enjoy the privilege of buying and selling, or do I choose possible death by refusing to receive the mark?*

For many, this decision shall be extremely excruciating. This moment will be eerily similar to what the early Christian Saints experienced, when a decision in favor of Christ meant certain death in the coliseum of Rome. For some, the thought of being able to maintain their worldly pleasures and possessions shall cause them to support the beast. Others, being more concerned with their relationship with God and His promise of eternal life and exaltation, will choose death.

Ironically, those who think they are choosing life by being able to buy and sell, shall lose their lives when the wrath of God is poured out upon the wicked, and their decision shall torment them for the rest of eternity. While those who choose death shall enjoy life with God in the eternal mansions of heaven.

> *11 And the smoke of their torment ascendeth up for ever and ever: and they have no rest day nor night, who worship the beast and his image, and whosoever receiveth the mark of his name.*[30]

What words of encouragement were given to those who will remain steadfast in keeping the commandments of God?

---

30. Rev. 14:11

The angel encourages the Saints to have patience, keep the commandments of God, and have faith in Jesus. Then came a voice from heaven saying, blessed are the dead who die in the Lord from *henceforth*, for they shall rest from their labours and their works shall follow them.

> *12 Here is the patience of the saints: here are they that keep the commandments of God, and the faith of Jesus.*
> *13 And I heard a voice from heaven saying unto me, Write, Blessed are the dead which die in the Lord from henceforth: Yea, saith the Spirit, that they may rest from their labours; and their works do follow them.[31]*

Is the main harvest about to begin?

In heaven, John sees the Son of Man (Savior) holding a sharp sickle in readiness to initiate the main harvest. On earth, Satan has the world divided into two camps, those who have *taken* on the mark of the beast, versus those who have *not*.[32] Soon the word is given that it is time to reap, and the "strange work" of God begins to unfold.[33]

Since the sounding of the seventh trump, Christ has taken control. At some point in time, the righteous must be separated from the wicked. In His infinite wisdom, the Lord shall do just that. By knowing the mind of His opponent and his need for power, greed, and control, the Lord shall allow an unwitting Satan and his cohorts, the beast and false prophet, to bring to pass the main harvest of the children of God.

> *14 And I looked, and behold a white cloud, and upon the cloud one sat like unto the Son of man, having on his head a golden crown, and in his hand a sharp sickle.*
> *15 And another angel came out of the temple, crying with a loud voice to him that sat on the cloud, Thrust in thy*

31. Rev. 14:12, 13
32. See Rev. 13:16
33. See Isaiah 28:21

sickle, and reap: for the time is come for thee to reap; for the harvest of the earth is ripe.
16 And he that sat on the cloud thrust in his sickle on the earth; and the earth was reaped.[34]

What will happen to those individuals who follow the beast?

Now that the harvest is complete with the wheat in the barn and the tares bundled and ready to be burned, John sees another angel come out of the temple carrying a sharp sickle. This angel is ordered to reap (by fire) the grapes of the earth. The grapes represent the beast, the false prophet, and all those who unite with the beast by taking upon them his mark.

This shall begin at Armageddon when the world shall join in battle against the God of Heaven. Here is where the wicked shall be cleansed from off the face of the earth, and the blood from this battle will flow over much of the soil of Israel: then God shall remember the iniquities of Babylon (the Kingdom of Satan) and reward her double according to her works.

17 And another angel came out of the temple which is in heaven, he also having a sharp sickle.
18 And another angel came out from the altar, which had power over fire; and cried with a loud cry to him that had the sharp sickle, saying, Thrust in thy sharp sickle, and gather the clusters of the vine of the earth; for her grapes are fully ripe.
19 And the angel thrust in his sickle into the earth, and gathered the vine of the earth, and cast it into the great winepress of the wrath of God.
20 And the winepress was trodden without the city, and blood came out of the winepress, even unto the horse

---

34. Rev. 14:14-16

bridles, by the space of a thousand and six hundred furlongs.[35]

It is important to know that these preceding scriptures provide only an overview, specific details relating to these events shall be covered in the succeeding chapters.

---

35. Rev. 14:17-20

15

Seven Vials

Having completed the overview, John is provided with some additional details concerning the conflict between the beast and the followers of Christ. As John looks, he sees a special group of Saints standing in the Kingdom of Heaven having received exaltation and glory for overcoming the image, mark, and number of the beast. He is also shown the behind scenes preparation, as the seven angels get ready to release their vials of God's wrath upon the nations of the earth.

Who are these Saints who have overcome the image, mark, and number of the beast?

These are the Saints who were *not* caught up to heaven, during the resurrection of the *elect*. Just of the thought of being left on earth, after many of their friends and loved one's were taken, must have been devastating. The feeling that all was lost, along with ever achieving any hope for a better life, must have penetrated every heart to the very core.

Nevertheless, all was *not* lost. God, in His infinite wisdom, had devised a plan whereby those who missed the resurrection of the *elect* had the opportunity (if they changed their ways) to still be a part of the resurrection of the first fruits. These are the followers of Christ who maintain their allegiance to Him by *not* taking on the mark of the beast; however, it shall require great suffering, even to the forfeiture of their mortal lives.

> *1 And I saw another sign in heaven, great and marvellous, seven angels having the seven last plagues; for in them is filled up the wrath of God.*
>
> *2 And I saw as it were a sea of glass mingled with fire: and them that had gotten the victory over the beast, and over his image, and over his mark, and over the number of his name, stand on the sea of glass, having the harps of God.*
>
> *3 And they sing the song of Moses the servant of God, and the song of the Lamb, saying, Great and marvellous are thy works, Lord God Almighty; just and true are thy ways, thou King of saints.*
>
> *4 Who shall not fear thee, O Lord, and glorify thy name? For thou only art holy: for all nations shall come and worship before thee; for thy judgments are made manifest.*[1]

After the seven angels came out of the heavenly temple, why was the temple closed?

As John looked, he sees the heavenly temple fill with smoke from the glory of God, and no man is able to *enter* into the temple, until the seven plagues of the seven angels are fulfilled. The reason for this is, that no other individuals shall be resur-

---

1. Rev. 15:1-4

rected into heaven until the seven angels have completed their missions.

> 5 And after that I looked, and, behold, the temple of the tabernacle of the testimony in heaven was opened:
> 6 And the seven angels came out of the temple, having the seven plagues, clothed in pure and white linen, and having their breasts girded with golden girdles.
> 7 And one of the four beasts gave unto the seven angels seven golden vials full of the wrath of God, who liveth for ever and ever.
> 8 And the temple was filled with smoke from the glory of God, and from his power; and no man was able to enter into the temple, till the seven plagues of the seven angels were fulfilled.[2]

---

2. Rev. 15:5-8

16

The Judgment Begins

At this point in time, many months will have passed
since the sounding of the seventh trumpet. The
beast and the false prophet, having overcome
most of their opponents, shall think they are in complete control
of the world.[1] However, events are about to change.

The wrath of God that fell upon the world prior to the sounding of the seventh trumpet is minuscule compared to what will
soon take place. Now the seven angels are ready to pour their
plagues upon the wicked. These plagues are designed to emulate
the type of pain the adversary and his minions have afflicted
upon the followers of Christ.

Yet, despite the great suffering that shall occur, the wicked
shall continue to blaspheme God by not repenting of their sins.
Then, as the time runs out for the gospel to be carried to the nations of the earth, time will also run out for Satan and his rulers
to dominate the world. With the words *"It is done"* ringing from
the throne of justice, the arm of the Lord shall fall, *first* upon

---

1. See Rev. 13:4-8

the armies of Satan gathered at a place called Armageddon, and *then* upon Babylon and the world at large.

Has the time finally arrived?

From the temple, John hears a voice give the final word that shall initiate the destruction of the wicked.

> *1 And I heard a great voice out of the temple saying to the seven angels, Go your ways, and pour out the vials of the wrath of God upon the earth.[2]*

What happens when the first vial is poured out?

When the first angel pours his vial upon the earth, there falls an offensive and grievous sore upon the men who have worshipped the beast by taking on his mark. Notice how this plague, when dispensed upon the wicked, shall mirror their offense. For example, since the wicked accepted the mark of the beast, they in turn, shall receive a mark (grievous sore) upon their skin.

> *2 And the first went, and poured out his vial upon the earth; and there fell a noisome and grievous sore upon the men which had the mark of the beast, and upon them which worshipped his image.[3]*

When the second vial is poured out, what will occur?

As the second angel empties his vial, the sea becomes as blood and every living soul dies in the sea. Thus, this angel shall initiate the same kind of plague used by the Lord to help free the Hebrews from the hands of the Egyptians. *"And he (Aaron)*

2. Rev. 16:1
3. Rev. 16:2

lifted up the rod, and smote the waters that were in the river, in the sight of Pharaoh, and in the sight of his servants; and all the waters that were in the river were turned to blood."[4]

> *3 And the second angel poured out his vial upon the sea; and it became as the blood of a dead man: and every living soul died in the sea.*[5]

What will ensue when the third angel pours his vial upon the earth?

All the rivers and fountains are turned to blood, and the result shall be the same as during the time of Moses, *"And the fish that was in the river died; and the river stank, and the Egyptians would not drink of the water of the river; and there was blood throughout all the land of Egypt."*[6]

> *4 And the third angel poured out his vial upon the rivers and fountains of waters; and they became blood.*[7]

Why will God turn the waters of the earth to blood?

The reason, John is told, is that the beast and his followers shall shed the blood of the Saints and prophets. Consequently, God shall be justified in giving them blood to drink.

> *5 And I heard the angel of the waters say, Thou art righteous, O Lord, which art, and wast, and shalt be, because thou hast judged thus.*
> *6 For they have shed the blood of saints and prophets, and thou hast given them blood to drink; for they are worthy.*

---

4. Exodus 7:20   6. Exodus 7:21
5. Rev. 16:3   7. Rev. 16:4

7 And I heard another out of the altar say, Even so, Lord
God Almighty, true and righteous are thy judgments.[8]

How will the fourth plague torment man?

As the fourth angel empties his vial, men are scorched with
great heat. Thus, as the followers of the beast scorched the righteous with fire and heat from weapons of war, they *in turn* shall
be scorched by fire and great heat. However, they shall still not
repent and submit to the God of Heaven.

8 And the fourth angel poured out his vial upon the sun;
and power was given unto him to scorch men with fire.
9 And men were scorched with great heat, and blasphemed
the name of God, which hath power over these plagues:
and they repented not to give him glory.[9]

What happened as the fifth angel poured out his vial?

The seat of the kingdom of the beast is full of darkness. As
the beast stifled the light of the gospel of Christ, the Lord shall
bring darkness upon the beast and his kingdom. This darkness
shall produce hate, misery, and despair, but they will still blame
God for all their misery.

10 And the fifth angel poured out his vial upon the seat of
the beast; and his kingdom was full of darkness; and they
gnawed their tongues for pain,
11 And blasphemed the God of heaven because of their
pains and their sores, and repented not of their deeds.[10]

---

8. Rev. 16:5-7
9. Rev. 16:8, 9
10. Rev. 16:10, 11

What will the sixth vial cause to happen?

When this vial is poured out upon the great river Euphrates, it shall open the way for the armies of the world to be destroyed. John is shown that the beast and the false prophet shall send emissaries to the kings of the world to gather them to battle.

These unclean spirits shall represent Satan, the beast, and the false prophet. They shall go forth unto the kings of the earth to gain their support in going to battle. For justification, the emissaries will probably say, *if we destroy the nation of Israel and their Holy Temple our fortunes shall change and all will be well*. Their plea will be successful and two hundred million men shall prepare to march into battle.[11]

> *12 And the sixth angel poured out his vial upon the great river Euphrates; and the water thereof was dried up, that the way of the kings of the east might be prepared.*
>
> *13 And I saw three unclean spirits like frogs come out of the mouth of the dragon, and out of the mouth of the beast, and out of the mouth of the false prophet.*
>
> *14 For they are the spirits of devils, working miracles, which go forth unto the kings of the earth and of the whole world, to gather them to the battle of that great day of God Almighty.[12]*

Will there be one last warning?

The Lord shall give one last warning by saying, *Behold, I come as a thief*. This warning shall be ignored by the beast and his followers. Truly, the final coming of the Lord shall be as a thief because, due to their wickedness, the beast and his followers shall be blind in their ability to interpret scripture.

---

11. See Rev. 9:16
12. Rev. 16:12-14

Also embedded within this warning is a message to the Saints. They are to carry on, and if they shall keep their garments clean from the sins of the world, then all shall be well. Though the beast and his followers shall be stunned when the Lord makes His appearance, the followers of Christ shall not be surprised. By watching and knowing the signs of the times, the Saints (located in cities of refuge) shall know when His arrival is very near.

> 15 Behold, I come as a thief. Blessed is he that watcheth, and keepeth his garments, lest he walk naked, and they see his shame.[13]

Where will this final battle be fought?

These armies shall meet their destiny in a place north of Jerusalem called Megiddo, or Armageddon. This is where the Lord shall gather the armies of the world.

> 16 And he gathered them together into a place called in the Hebrew tongue Armageddon.[14]

When the seventh angel pours out his vial, what will happen?

This shall place in motion the means whereby the remainder of the wicked can be destroyed. God shall declare *"It is done;"* meaning the last series of events will soon begin.

Concerning the armies gathered at Armageddon and all those who fight against Jerusalem, the Lord shall smite these forces in such a way that their flesh, eyes, and tongue shall consume away while they are yet standing on their feet. This is reminiscent of

---

13. Rev. 16:15
14. Rev. 16:16

how individuals met their demise in the bombing of Hiroshima during the Second World War. Those individuals not killed in this manner shall begin to fight amongst themselves until many shall be destroyed. *"And it shall come to pass in that day, that I will seek to destroy all the nations that come against Jerusalem."*[15]

"And this shall be the plague wherewith the LORD will smite all the people that have fought against Jerusalem; Their flesh shall consume away while they stand upon their feet, and their eyes shall consume away in their holes, and their tongue shall consume away in their mouth. And it shall come to pass in that day, that a great tumult from the LORD shall be among them; and they shall lay hold every one on the hand of his neighbour, and his hand shall rise up against the hand of his neighbour. And Judah also shall fight at Jerusalem; and the wealth of all the heathen round about shall be gathered together, gold, and silver, and apparel, in great abundance. And so shall be the plague of the horse, of the mule, of the camel, and of the ass, and of all the beasts that shall be in these tents, as this plague."[16]

Following this, a great earthquake shall occur, it *will* be the greatest earthquake known to man. During this quake, *the* great city (*Jerusalem*)[17] shall be divided into three parts. Then, the cities of the nations shall fall, and the great Babylon (Kingdom of Satan) shall come into remembrance before God, to receive the fierceness of His wrath. Subsequently, the islands shall flee and mountains shall be made low, and a great plague of lethal hail shall fall upon men.

> *17 And the seventh angel poured out his vial into the air; and there came a great voice out of the temple of heaven, from the throne, saying, It is done.*

15. Zech. 12:9
16. Zech. 14:12-15
17. Rev. 11:8

18 And there were voices, and thunders, and lightnings; and there was a great earthquake, such as was not since men were upon the earth, so mighty an earthquake, and so great.

19 And the great city was divided into three parts, and the cities of the nations fell: and great Babylon came in remembrance before God, to give unto her the cup of the wine of the fierceness of his wrath.

20 And every island fled away, and the mountains were not found.

21 And there fell upon men a great hail out of heaven, every stone about the weight of a talent: and men blasphemed God because of the plague of the hail; for the plague thereof was exceeding great.[18]

---

18. Rev. 16:17-21

17

Babylon, Beast, & Ten Kings

Following the presentation regarding the seven plagues and the main harvest, John is allowed to see a more detailed view pertaining to the kingdom of Satan. To enable John to comprehend the mystery of the whore called, *Babylon the Great*, he sees a woman who sits upon a scarlet colored beast, having seven heads and ten horns. An angel then identifies each individual demonic entity and explains how they shall interact with one another to war against the Lamb of God.

In this vision, John discovers that the kingdom of Satan is divided into two parts, the secular side, which (as previously mentioned) comprise the depraved political kingdoms of the world, and then, the church of Satan, which is called, *Babylon the Great*. Just before the Second Coming, unaware that God shall put it in their hearts to do His bidding, these two demonic entities (the *wicked political kingdoms of the world* and *Babylon the Great*) shall fight amongst themselves, until Babylon the Great is destroyed and burned with fire.

Regarding the judgment of the great whore, what did the angel say to John?

An angel told John to come and he would show him the judgment of the great whore that sits upon many waters.

> *1 And there came one of the seven angels which had the seven vials, and talked with me, saying unto me, Come hither; I will shew unto thee the judgment of the great whore that sitteth upon many waters:*
> *2 With whom the kings of the earth have committed fornication, and the inhabitants of the earth have been made drunk with the wine of her fornication.[1]*

Why is the kingdom of Satan divided into two groups?

It is divided in this manner because it will help the Devil in the battle for the souls of all mankind.

The first group includes those individuals who are either atheist or agnostic. The atheist believes that there is no God. The agnostic believes that whether God exists is not known and probably cannot be known. This group constitutes the worldly or secular arm of the kingdom of Satan.

The second group is made up of individuals who harbor the desire to worship a higher power. This group is the ecclesiastical or religious arm of Satan's kingdom. Long ago, Satan realized that if he could harness man's yearning to worship a higher power, he could accomplish two goals. First, he could exploit this craving to build his kingdom and second, he could

---

1. Rev. 17:1, 2

use it to keep individuals from discovering the saving truths and ordinances of the real Church of Jesus Christ, as validated by the apostle Paul when said there is only, *"One Lord, one faith, one baptism"*.[2]

How would Satan do this? He would simply start his own church... the church of Satan. His church would contain just enough of the teachings of Christ so as to pacify its members into believing that they really did belong to the true Church of Jesus Christ. And if the teachings of one church did not satisfy their desires, he would gladly provide other churches with differing beliefs to meet their wishes as well. Satan was willing to provide anything to anybody as long as they paid their tithes and offerings into his coffers. Over the course of many generations, some of his churches became extremely wealthy, thus creating a seedbed where lying, cheating, bribery, stealing, greed, blasphemy, corruption, blackmail, revenge, and even murder could flourish as individuals clawed there way upward in search of power, strength, and glory. All this was done under the guise of religion.

This is what John sees when he is carried away into the wilderness. The woman he observes sitting upon a scarlet colored beast represents this church of Satan. How the woman is arrayed in purple and scarlet colors and decked with gold, pearls, and precious stones symbolizes the great wealth his church shall accumulate over the years. The golden cup in her hand (full of abominations and filthiness) stands for the totality of crimes the church shall perpetrate to help Satan and his followers stay in power. This is why the name, "MYSTERY, BABYLON THE GREAT, THE MOTHER OF HARLOTS AND ABOMINATION OF THE EARTH" was written across her forehead.

Even more appalling is the next scene that John witnesses, when he sees the woman drunken with the blood of the Saints and martyrs of Jesus Christ. What is John's reaction to this? All

2. Eph. 4:5

he can do is look with great astonishment as he realizes just how deeply this church shall be involved in the deaths of his beloved brethren and followers of Christ.

> *3 So he carried me away in the spirit into the wilderness: and I saw a woman sit upon a scarlet coloured beast, full of names of blasphemy, having seven heads and ten horns. 4 And the woman was arrayed in purple and scarlet colour, and decked with gold and precious stones and pearls, having a golden cup in her hand full of abominations and filthiness of her fornication:*
> *5 And upon her forehead was a name written, MYSTERY, BABYLON THE GREAT, THE MOTHER OF HARLOTS AND ABOMINATIONS OF THE EARTH.*
> *6 And I saw the woman drunken with the blood of the saints, and with the blood of the martyrs of Jesus: and when I saw her, I wondered with great admiration.[3]*

Concerning the mystery of the beast, seven heads and ten horns, what did the angel say?

The angel informs John that he would now learn the mystery of the beast, and the seven heads and ten horns.

> *7 And the angel said unto me, Wherefore didst thou marvel? I will tell thee the mystery of the woman, and of the beast that carrieth her, which hath the seven heads and ten horns.[4]*

Who is the beast that John saw ascending out of the bottomless pit?

The beast John sees, is none other than Satan himself. This is evidenced by the fact that he shall have access to and from the bottomless pit and then, eventually, shall go into perdition.[5]

---

3. Rev. 17:3-6
4. Rev. 17:7
5. Rev. 9:11

The reason he is given the nickname, as the beast — *that was, and is not, and yet is* – pertains to his status in premortal life. Before the war in heaven, Satan was known as Lucifer, which means *light bearer* or *the shining one,* thus indicating he once held a very high position of prominence and authority in the Kingdom of God. With this position came great respect and veneration. After his rebellion and fall, he lost that position.[6] However, the time shall come (after the seventh king arrives on stage) that Satan shall again enjoy great adoration and glory, as will be explained shortly. Thus the name — *the beast that was, and is not, and yet is* — simply refers to this cycle in Satan's existence.

Due to their allegiance to the beast, multitudes of his follow-ers shall be thrust down to hell because they did not have their name written in the book of life. When they finally meet the beast (Satan), they shall look upon him with wonder, thinking, *"How could this one person make the earth and kingdoms tremble?"*[7]

Eventually, he shall be cast into perdition, which is a place reserved for the impure. It is also a location where its inhabitants are separated from all things pertaining to righteousness, and then tormented forever (as if in a lake of fire and brimstone).

> 8 *The beast that thou sawest was, and is not; and shall ascend out of the bottomless pit, and go into perdition: and they that dwell on the earth shall wonder, whose names were not written in the book of life from the foundation of the world, when they behold the beast that was, and is not, and yet is.*[8]

---

6. See Isa. 14:12-20
7. Isa. 14:16
8. Rev. 17:8

What do the seven heads represent?

The seven heads, John is told, are seven mountains on which the woman sits. One of the characteristics of some mountains is that they have the ability to raise themselves above the plain by means of internal volcanic forces.[9]

In like manner, certain individuals have been born with internal abilities that enable them to perform great feats of accomplishments for themselves and others. Thus, these seven heads are seven mountains (individuals) who, through their actions, have raised the woman (church of Satan) above the plain in terms of power, prestige, and prominence. Therefore, whatever success the woman enjoys, truly rests upon the shoulders of these seven individuals.

> 9 And here is the mind which hath wisdom. The seven heads are seven mountains, on which the woman sitteth.[10]

Who are the seven kings?

Concerning the seven kings, John discovers that five had already died, one is still alive (during John's time), and one is yet to be born.

He is also told that there would be an *eighth* king, but in some way this eighth king would be part of the seven. What is the answer to this dilemma? This eighth king is Satan, as evidence by the fact that he is *the beast that was, and is not, even he is and will go into perdition.* In some miraculous way, Satan shall be able to manifest himself vicariously through the seventh king. This is how he shall, once again, enjoy the power, strength, and glory he is so earnestly seeking. And thus, it shall be said he is the eighth, but is still part of the seven.

---

9. Strong's Concordance of the Bible, Greek Dictionary of the New Testament, Page 52, Reference: 3735 & 3733
10. Rev. 17:9

10 And there are seven kings: five are fallen, and one is,
and the other is not yet come; and when he cometh, he
must continue a short space.
11 And the beast that was, and is not, even he is the eighth,
and is of the seven, and goeth into perdition.[11]

And the ten horns which John saw, who are they?

The ten horns are ten kings, who have received no kingdom
as yet, but shall receive power (as kings) for one hour with
the seventh beast. Since the ten horns represent ten kings, it is
important to know when and how they shall interact with the
seventh beast. Each king is in command of a great nation, when
all ten kings act as one, they shall have control over most of the
world. The beast shall possess the charisma to convince these
leaders to give their power and strength to him. His message
shall be simply: *"If we work together, we can control the world.*
If we work separately, we can never achieve that goal, and may
even end up destroying one another." Since they all possess the
same desire for power, strength, and glory, they shall decide in
favor of the beast's proposal. This agreement shall take effect,
when the Savior assumes the reins of power as the seventh
trump sounds.

The seventh beast and the ten kings shall make war with
the Lamb (Jesus Christ), and the Lamb shall overcome them.
Initially, it shall appear that the Saints of God cannot prevail
against the beast and ten kings. Their numbers shall be very few
due to the wicked and oppressive tactics used by the enemy.
However, because of the righteousness of the Saints, they shall
be shielded by the power of the Lamb. Eventually, the wrath
of God shall be poured out upon His detractors and the Lamb
shall overcome them.

---

11. Rev. 17:10, 11

*12 And the ten horns which thou sawest are ten kings,
which have received no kingdom as yet; but receive power
as kings one hour with the beast.
13 These have one mind, and shall give their power and
strength unto the beast.
14 These shall make war with the Lamb, and the Lamb
shall overcome them: for he is Lord of lords, and King of
kings: and they that are with him are called, and chosen,
and faithful.[12]*

Regarding the waters that John saw, what do they represent?

The waters represent peoples, multitudes, nations, and tongues, of different people. Thus, when the angel informs John that the whore sits upon many waters (peoples, multitudes, nations, and tongues), he is (in essence) saying that the large and small churches that constitute the church of Satan (Babylon the great, the mother of harlots and abominations) have become established throughout the world.

*15 And he saith unto me, The waters which thou sawest,
where the whore sitteth, are peoples, and multitudes, and
nations, and tongues.[13]*

What will the ten horns do to the whore?

The ten horns (ten kings) shall hate the whore, and make her desolate by burning her with fire.

When these ten kings initially join with the seventh beast, it shall be to realize their dream of controlling the world. However, as the wrath of God is poured out, and they see their dreams evaporate before their eyes, it shall dredge up feelings of intense

---

12. Rev. 17:12-14
13. Rev. 17:15

hatred and a smoldering desire for revenge on anything that even hints of religion. In due course, they shall turn their attention to the whore, who represents the ecclesiastical side of Satan's kingdom and burn her with fire. This they shall do without ever realizing that they both work for the same master.

Who is really watching over these events? It is an all-powerful, all seeing, and all knowing Father in Heaven executing His plan of sifting the righteous from the wicked to bring to pass the immortality and eternal life of man.

> *16 And the ten horns which thou sawest upon the beast, these shall hate the whore, and shall make her desolate and naked, and shall eat her flesh, and burn her with fire. 17 For God hath put in their hearts to fulfil his will, and to agree, and give their kingdom unto the beast, until the words of God shall be fulfilled.*[14]

So what great city, which reigns over the kings of the earth, will symbolize the woman (church of Satan) during the last days?

This city shall be *Rome*, the eternal city of Italy, located just off the coast of the Mediterranean Sea. As the worldly or secular arm of the kingdom of Satan needs a seat of power to grow and flourish; in like manner, the religious or ecclesiastical side also requires a seat of power to develop and increase his church.

Periodically, over the centuries, Rome has displayed many of the characteristics of the church of Satan. Why? First, this city has corrupted many of the kings of the earth. Next, she has accumulated great wealth and is literally decked with gold, pearls, and precious stones. Having spawned many generations of smaller churches of Satan, she is the mother of harlots and

---

14. Rev. 17:16, 17

abominations of the earth. Her golden cup is filled with abomination and filthiness of her fornications of what she had to do to achieve her fame, wealth, and power. Finally, this is the city that is drunk with the blood of the Saints and martyrs of Jesus Christ. Thus, when the time comes for the symbol of the whore to be burned, Rome is the city that shall receive special attention, and then the rest of the church of Satan shall be given its reward.

> *18 And the woman which thou sawest is that great city, which reigneth over the kings of the earth.*[15]

---

15. Rev. 17:18

18

The Fall of Babylon

N ow that John understands the nature of Babylon,
the angel is prepared to show him a close up view
of the terrible destruction that shall take place.
John sees a mighty angel declare the judgment on Babylon.
However, before this happens, the righteous are urged to depart
this way of life, so as not to partake of her sins.

Having lived a glorious life filled with wickedness, depravity,
and corruption, Babylon shall now experience the wrath of God.
As a penalty for causing the death of so many disciples of Christ,
her pain and suffering will be doubled, and then she shall be
thrown violently to the ground never to rise again. Though some
profiteers of Babylon will express great remorse, the angels shall
rejoice because the God of Heaven and Earth hath avenged His
Saints.

Why is the destruction of Babylon necessary?

Babylon the great is fallen, announces the angel to John, meaning the decision has been made to destroy Babylon. The reason behind this decision is due to her immoral association with the kings and merchants of the earth for monetary gain.

> *1 And after these things I saw another angel come down from heaven, having great power; and the earth was lightened with his glory.*
>
> *2 And he cried mightily with a strong voice, saying, Babylon the great is fallen, is fallen, and is become the habitation of devils, and the hold of every foul spirit, and a cage of every unclean and hateful bird.*
>
> *3 For all nations have drunk of the wine of the wrath of her fornication, and the kings of the earth have committed fornication with her, and the merchants of the earth are waxed rich through the abundance of her delicacies.[1]*

What must happen before the destruction can begin?

John hears a voice from heaven warning the Saints to come out of Babylon. Thus when the angel says, *come out of her, my people, that ye be not partakers of her sins*, it is a warning for the Saints, Gentiles, and Israelites to flee from any type of Babylonian influence and go to their predesignated city of refuge as mentioned in chapter 14.

> *4 And I heard another voice from heaven, saying, Come out of her, my people, that ye be not partakers of her sins, and that ye receive not of her plagues.[2]*

How terrible is the destruction of Babylon?

---

1. Rev. 18:1-3
2. Rev. 18:4

The angel reminds John that God is aware of the wickedness of Babylon and that He shall not only reward her as she rewarded the Saints but will double that reward. When this destruction occurs, Babylon shall be astounded because she thinks she is so great that nothing can ever happen to her.

> *5 For her sins have reached unto heaven, and God hath remembered her iniquities.*
> *6 Reward her even as she rewarded you, and double unto her double according to her works: in the cup which she hath filled fill to her double.*
> *7 How much she hath glorified herself, and lived deliciously, so much torment and sorrow give her: for she saith in her heart, I sit a queen, and am no widow, and shall see no sorrow.*[3]

Concerning the destruction of Babylon, how long will it take?

John is told her destruction will come in one day, and she shall be burned by fire.

> *8 Therefore shall her plagues come in one day, death, and mourning, and famine; and she shall be utterly burned with fire: for strong is the Lord God who judgeth her.*[4]

What will the various world leaders do when Babylon is destroyed?

John is shown that the kings of the earth, who have richly benefited from their association with Babylon, shall mourn for her, as they see the smoke of her destruction billowing skyward.

---

3. Rev. 18:5-7
4. Rev. 18:8

9 And the kings of the earth, who have committed fornication and lived deliciously with her, shall bewail her, and lament for her, when they shall see the smoke of her burning,
10 Standing afar off for the fear of her torment, saying, Alas, alas, that great city Babylon, that mighty city! for in one hour is thy judgment come.[5]

Why will the merchants of the earth mourn for her?

The reason the merchants are mourning, is not for the love of the city, but because of greed. In other words, who will now buy their merchandise?

11 And the merchants of the earth shall weep and mourn over her; for no man buyeth their merchandise any more:
12 The merchandise of gold, and silver, and precious stones, and of pearls, and fine linen, and purple, and silk, and scarlet, and all thyine wood, and all manner vessels of ivory, and all manner vessels of most precious wood, and of brass, and iron, and marble,
13 And cinnamon, and odours, and ointments, and frankincense, and wine, and oil, and fine flour, and wheat, and beasts, and sheep, and horses, and chariots, and slaves, and souls of men.
14 And the fruits that thy soul lusted after are departed from thee, and all things which were dainty and goodly are departed from thee, and thou shalt find them no more at all.
15 The merchants of these things, which were made rich by her, shall stand afar off for the fear of her torment, weeping and wailing,
16 And saying, Alas, alas, that great city, that was clothed in fine linen, and purple, and scarlet, and decked with gold, and precious stones, and pearls![6]

---

5. Rev. 18:9, 10
6. Rev. 18:11-16

Regarding the shipmasters and sailors, why are they mourning?

John sees that their mourning is due to the financial loss they will now incur. *How are we going to live, and what will happen to us?* These will be just some of the questions they must now address.

> *17 For in one hour so great riches is come to nought. And every shipmaster, and all the company in ships, and sailors, and as many as trade by sea, stood afar off,*
> *18 And cried when they saw the smoke of her burning, saying, What city is like unto this great city!*
> *19 And they cast dust on their heads, and cried, weeping and wailing, saying, Alas, alas, that great city, wherein were made rich all that had ships in the sea by reason of her costliness! For in one hour is she made desolate.[7]*

Why is heaven rejoicing over the fall of Babylon?

They are rejoicing because the end of wickedness has finally arrived as God takes vengeance for the slaying of His prophets, Saints, and disciples. Thus, Babylon shall be thrown down, and then burned, to rise no more.

> *20 Rejoice over her, thou heaven, and ye holy apostles and prophets; for God hath avenged you on her.*
> *21 And a mighty angel took up a stone like a great millstone, and cast it into the sea, saying, Thus with violence shall that great city Babylon be thrown down, and shall be found no more at all.*
> *22 And the voice of harpers, and musicians, and of pipers, and trumpeters, shall be heard no more at all in thee; and no craftsman, of whatsoever craft he be, shall be found*

---

7. Rev. 18:17-19

any more in thee; and the sound of a millstone shall be heard no more at all in thee;

23 And the light of a candle shall shine no more at all in thee; and the voice of the bridegroom and of the bride shall be heard no more at all in thee: for thy merchants were the great men of the earth; for by thy sorceries were all nations deceived.

24 And in her was found the blood of prophets, and of saints, and of all that were slain upon the earth.[8]

---

8. Rev. 18:20-24

19

The Wedding, Marriage Supper, & the Final Coming

After observing what the Lord has planned for Babylon, John sees other angels making preparations for the marriage supper of the Lamb. He sees the armies of the world converging at Armageddon to fight the greatest battle in the history of the world.

Suddenly, the vision changes as a rider on a white horse comes into view with the name King of Kings and Lord of Lords written on His thigh. Thus, ending a war that has been raging for over six thousand years, Jesus Christ, wearing crowns of victory upon His head and followed by His host of Saints, shall descend upon the army of Satan with the fierceness and wrath that only an Almighty God can muster. Hence, the beast and false prophet are taken and cast into a lake of fire, and the remnant slain by the word of the Lord.

Why is there joy in heaven?

John sees twenty-four elders, four beasts, and multitudes of Saints rejoicing and expressing their thankfulness to God for being allowed to participate in a sacred heavenly event that shall soon occur.

> *1 And after these things I heard a great voice of much people in heaven, saying, Alleluia; Salvation, and glory, and honour, and power, unto the Lord our God:*
>
> *2 For true and righteous are his judgments: for he hath judged the great whore, which did corrupt the earth with her fornication, and hath avenged the blood of his servants at her hand.*
>
> *3 And again they said, Alleluia. And her smoke rose up for ever and ever.*
>
> *4 And the four and twenty elders and the four beasts fell down and worshipped God that sat on the throne, saying, Amen; Alleluia.*
>
> *5 And a voice came out of the throne, saying, Praise our God, all ye his servants, and ye that fear him, both small and great.*
>
> *6 And I heard as it were the voice of a great multitude, and as the voice of many waters, and as the voice of mighty thunderings, saying, Alleluia: for the Lord God omnipotent reigneth.[1]*

What sacred event is about to happen?

The time has arrived, John is told, for the marriage to take place between the Lamb of God and His bride, which is the body of faithful Saints who make up the Church of Jesus Christ.

---

1. Rev. 19:1-6

7 Let us be glad and rejoice, and give honour to him: for the marriage of the Lamb is come, and his wife hath made herself ready.[2]

What type of clothing will be required for this wedding?

Only those who are dressed in clean white linen shall participate in this marriage ceremony.

8 And to her was granted that she should be arrayed in fine linen, clean and white: for the fine linen is the righteousness of saints.[3]

Regarding the marriage feast, what was John told to write?

He is to write, blessed are they who are called unto the marriage supper of the Lamb. Thus, only those who have a testimony of Jesus Christ shall participate in this feast.

9 And he saith unto me, Write, Blessed are they which are called unto the marriage supper of the Lamb. And he saith unto me, These are the true sayings of God.
10 And I fell at his feet to worship him. And he said unto me, See thou do it not: I am thy fellowservant, and of thy brethren that have the testimony of Jesus: worship God: for the testimony of Jesus is the spirit of prophecy.[4]

At this time, what crises will distress the inhabitants of Jerusalem?

---

2. Rev. 19:7
3. Rev. 19:8
4. Rev. 19:9, 10

The armies of all nations shall be locked in battle against the inhabitants of Jerusalem and much of the city shall be taken, the houses rifled, and women ravished. It shall be a dire time for Judah, for many shall think that the Lord has forsaken them.

> 2 For I will gather all nations against Jerusalem to battle; and the city shall be taken, and the houses rifled, and the women ravished; and half of the city shall go forth into captivity, and the residue of the people shall not be cut off from the city.[5]

How will the Lord step in to rescue His people?

Though the armies of many nations shall surround Jerusalem, Christ shall provide a way to escape. An earthquake shall suddenly occur and the Mount of Olives shall be divided. This shall create a great valley in which the children of Judah can flee towards Azal.

As they flee from their oppressors, the figure of a man shall appear, however, instead of joining their flight; He shall stand like a shepherd watching over His sheep. Compared to the frightened and terrified actions of the people, His calm demeanor will elicit curiosity. Someone will say, *"What are these wounds in thine hands?"* and He will say, *"Those with which I was wounded in the house of my friends."*[6] Then, the realization that this is Jesus Christ shall permeate into the consciousness of the crowd. And they shall look upon Him whom they have pierced, and they shall mourn for him, as one mourneth for his only son, and shall be in bitterness for him, as one that is in bitterness for his firstborn.[7]

It is important to understand that this appearance of Christ is *not* the main event of the Second Coming. His coming on a

---

5. Zech. 14:2
6. Zech. 13:6
7. See Zech. 12:9, 10

white horse in clouds of glory shall take place *after* they flee to
the valley of the mountains unto Azal.

> *4 And his feet shall stand in that day upon the mount of*
> *Olives, which is before Jerusalem on the east, and the*
> *mount of Olives shall cleave in the midst thereof toward the*
> *east and toward the west, and there shall be a very great*
> *valley; and half of the mountain shall remove toward the*
> *north, and half of it toward the south.*
> *5 And ye shall flee to the valley of the mountains; for the*
> *valley of the mountains shall reach unto Azal: yea, ye shall*
> *flee, like as ye fled from before the earthquake in the days*
> *of Uzziah king of Judah: and the LORD my God shall*
> *come, and all the saints with thee.*[8]

When the actual day arrives, what will it be like?

It will be a day when the sun shall go down, *yet there shall*
be no darkness. In other words, when night arrives it shall still
be light. It will be a day known only to the Lord and when He
comes, a fountain shall flow forth from under the house of the
Lord that shall water the valley of Shittum.[9] It shall be a day
when finally, there will be only one King and He shall be King
over all the earth.

> *6 And it shall come to pass in that day, that the light shall*
> *not be clear, nor dark:*
> *7 But it shall be one day which shall be known to the*
> *LORD, not day, nor night: but is shall come to pass, that*
> *at evening time it shall be light.*
> *8 And it shall be in that day, that living waters shall go*
> *out from Jerusalem; half of them toward the former sea,*
> *and half of them toward the hinder sea: in summer and*
> *in winter shall it be.*

---

8. Zech. 14:4, 5
9. Joel 3:18

9 And the LORD shall be king over all the earth: in that day shall there be one LORD, and his name one." [10]

What is THE event that all mankind has been waiting for since the days of Adam and Eve?

Up to this point, God has desperately tried to urge the vain, prideful, and wicked to repent. He has sent millions of missionaries to gather them as a hen gathereth her chickens under her wings, but to no avail. He has provided prophets, scriptures, and ministers; still no reaction. He has sent two witnesses into the streets of Jerusalem, in response, they were killed. He then allowed the seven thunders and the angels with the seven vials to shake the earth with lightnings, tempests, earthquakes, great hailstorms, famines, and pestilences in hopes of seeing some change for the better; still nothing worked. He has offered glory, honor, riches, and everlasting salvation to those who qualify for eternal life; only deafening silence was the result. Now the day has arrived, the cup of wrath is full and the arm of the Lord is ready to fall.

As mentioned previously, when the Lord opened the seventh seal, there was *silence* in heaven for about half an hour. [11] This *silence* preceded the sounding of the first trump that initiated the series of events that God hoped would instill a change of heart within His children. This *silence* was a type and shadow of what shall occur just before the Second Coming.

Therefore, again, *silence* shall reign in heaven for the space of half an hour. Soon the command shall be given, the heavens shall be *unfolded*, and the glory of the Lord shall be revealed. [12] Then all flesh shall see it together, as the Savior appears upon

---

10. Zech. 14:6-9
11. See Rev. 8:1
12. See Isa. 40:5

a white horse, wearing crowns of victory and clothed with a vesture (clothing) dipped in blood.

> *11 And I saw heaven opened, and behold a white horse; and he that sat upon him was called Faithful and True, and in righteousness he doth judge and make war.*
>
> *12 His eyes were as a flame of fire, and on his head were many crowns; and he had a name written, that no man knew, but he himself.*
>
> *13 And he was clothed with a vesture dipped in blood: and his name is called The Word of God.*[13]

Why will tears of joy flow with intense emotion?

In chapter 14 of this book, while describing the resurrection of the *"elect,"* the Savior explains to Matthew: *"Immediately after the tribulation of those days shall the sun be darkened, and the moon shall not give her light, and the stars shall fall from heaven, and powers of the heavens shall be shaken: And then shall appear the sign of the Son of man in heaven: and then shall all the tribes of the earth mourn, and they shall see the Son of man coming in the clouds of heaven with power and great glory. And he shall send his angels with a great sound of a trumpet, and they shall gather together his elect from the four winds, from one end of heaven to the other. Now learn a parable of the fig tree; When his branch is yet tender, and putteth forth leaves, ye know that summer is nigh: So likewise ye, when ye shall see all these things, know that it is near, even at the doors."*[14]

By using the word *"likewise,"* in essence, the Lord is saying, *"in like manner,"* thus implying that another resurrection will occur, which shall be similar to the resurrection of the *"elect."* This is *that* resurrection! These are *"they"* who were *"not"* resurrected with the *"elect"* but are still part of the first fruits.

---

13. Rev. 19:11-13
14. Matt. 24:29-33

In other words, this marks the moment when the *remnant*[15] of the first fruits of God, who *survive* the reign of the beast and false prophet, shall become one with the Savior, as a bride is one with her husband and shall become joint heirs of all the blessings that God the Father has in store for His Son and His bride.

This marriage shall take place as the Son of Man descends from heaven and is united with His faithful Saints. Those Saints *who are alive* shall be caught up to meet the Lord in the pillars of heaven, and *then the graves shall be opened, so that the rest of the dead in Christ,* who did *not* survive the reign of the beast and false prophet, can also rise to meet the Lord.

Thus, the Saints who are alive, shall be caught up to safety just before the arm of the Lord shall fall, much as in the days of Noah and Lot, *"And as it was in the days of Noe, so shall it be also in the days of the Son of man. They did eat, they drank, they married wives, they were given in marriage, until the day that Noe entered into the ark, and the flood came, and destroyed them all. Likewise also as it was in the days of Lot; they did eat, they drank, they brought, they sold, they planted, they builded; But the same day that Lot went out of Sodom it rained fire and brimstone from heaven, and destroyed them all. Even thus shall it be in the day when the Son of man is revealed. In that day, he which shall be upon the housetop, and his stuff in the house, let him not come down to take it away: and he that is in the field, let him likewise not return back. Remember Lot's wife. Whosoever shall seek to save his life shall lose it; and whosoever shall lose his life shall preserve it. I tell you, in that night there shall be two men in one bed; the one shall be taken, and the other shall be left. Two women shall be grinding together; the one shall be taken, and the other left. Two men shall be in the field; the one shall be taken, and the other left. And they answered and said unto him, Where, Lord? And he said unto them, Wheresoever*

---

15. Rev. 12:17

the body is, thither will the eagles be gathered together."[16] Therefore, these are the wise, depicted in the parable of the ten virgins who, *because they had oil in their lamps, were allowed to join with the bridegroom before the door to the bridal chamber was shut.*[17] Moreover, these are they who shall join the army of Saints as they follow the Savior upon white horses, clothed in fine linen, during His triumphal return to merge with the Kingdom of God on earth.

> *14 And the armies which were in heaven followed him upon white horses, clothed in fine linen, white and clean.*[18]

How will Christ overcome the wicked?

The *word* of the Lord, John is told, shall be like a two-edged sword, and Christ shall use a rod of iron to rule all nations.

> *15 And out of his mouth goeth a sharp sword, that with it he should smite the nations: and he shall rule them with a rod of iron: and he treadeth the winepress of the fierceness and wrath of Almighty God.*
>
> *16 And he hath on his vesture and on his thigh a name written, KING OF KINGS, AND LORD OF LORDS.*
>
> *17 And I saw an angel standing in the sun; and he cried with a loud voice, saying to all the fowls that fly in the midst of heaven, Come and gather yourselves together unto the supper of the great God;*
>
> *18 That ye may eat the flesh of kings, and the flesh of captains, and the flesh of mighty men, and the flesh of horses, and of them that sit on them, and the flesh of all men, both free and bond, both small and great.*

---

16. Luke 17:26-37
17. See Matt. 25:1-10
18. Rev. 19:14

19 And I saw the beast, and the kings of the earth, and
their armies, gathered together to make war against him
that sat on the horse, and against his army.[19]

What will happen to the beast and the false prophet?

John sees that the beast and the false prophet shall be taken and cast alive into a place where their punishment is compared to being confined in a lake of fire burning with sulfur.

20 And the beast was taken, and with him the false prophet
that wrought miracles before him, with which he deceived
them that had received the mark of the beast, and them that
worshipped his image. These both were cast alive into a
lake of fire burning with brimstone.[20]

How will the rest of the armies of Satan fare?

John describes the slaughter of the armies of Satan as being so great that he sees an angel calling to the fowls of the air to come and feast upon the flesh of all those who followed Satan.

21 And the remnant were slain with the sword of him
that sat upon the horse, which sword proceeded out of
his mouth: and all the fowls were filled with their flesh.[21]

---

19. Rev. 19:15-19
20. Rev. 19:20
21. Rev. 19:21

20

The Disposition of Satan & the Wicked

The Second Coming of the Lord has arrived, Armageddon has been fought, and Satan has lost. The beast and false prophet have been captured and imprisoned in a place where their souls shall be tormented forever. Satan is bound and cast into a pit. Those who did not worship the beast shall reign with Christ for a thousand years. While those who sided with Satan must wait, at least, a thousand years before they can be resurrected.

When the thousand years have expired, Satan shall, yet *again*, be allowed to tempt the children of God. Once more, the wrath of God shall fall upon Satan, and then he shall be thrown into the lake of fire to join the beast and false prophet and all who are not found in the book of life. Finally, John sees the dead stand before God. The books are opened and they are judged, each according to his or her works.

Who will capture Satan?

John sees an angel descend from heaven. This angel is holding a chain and the key to the bottomless pit. Satan is captured, bound with a chain, and shut away for a thousand years. During this time, his ability to deceive shall be taken away. After this thousand-year period expires, he shall be loosed for a short time.

> *1 And I saw an angel come down from heaven, having the key of the bottomless pit and a great chain in his hand.*
> *2 And he laid hold on the dragon, that old serpent, which is the Devil, and Satan, and bound him a thousand years,*
> *3 And cast him into the bottomless pit, and shut him up, and set a seal upon him, that he should deceive the nations no more, till the thousand years should be fulfilled: and after that he must be loosed a little season.*[1]

As the judgment begins, what did John see?

He is able to witness the judgment of those who were beheaded for being a witness of Jesus. As mentioned previously, the individuals who fall into this category, who are steadfast members of Christ's Church, shall obtain eternal life. While those who have not had the chance to hear the true and everlasting gospel shall receive that opportunity. This is why Peter said, *"For, for this cause was the gospel preached also to them that are dead, that they might be judged according to men in the flesh, but live according to God in the spirit."*[2] In either case, these honorable souls shall still be able to live and reign with Christ for a thousand years.

---

1. Rev. 20:1-3
2. 1 Peter 4:6

> *4 And I saw thrones, and they sat upon them, and judgment was given unto them: and I saw the souls of them that were beheaded for the witness of Jesus, and for the word of God, and which had not worshipped the beast, neither his image, neither had received his mark upon their foreheads, or in their hands; and they lived and reigned with Christ a thousand years.*[3]

Regarding the rest of the dead, what will happen to them?

The rest of the dead, the angel said, shall *not* be resurrected until the thousand years are finished. This is known as *"the second resurrection."* The statement, *"This is the first resurrection"* listed below, pertains only to the Saints who shall live with Christ for one thousand years.

> *5 But the rest of the dead lived not again until the thousand years were finished. This is the first resurrection.*[4]

Why are those Saints who take part in the first resurrection called blessed and holy, and what will happen to the wicked who are consigned to the second death?

The Saints who take part in the first resurrection are called blessed and holy because they shall become priests of God and Christ, and will reign with Him for a thousand years.

The second death refers to a type of spiritual death. In other words, it means to be spiritually cut off from the Lord, or any person, place, or thing, that involves holiness or righteousness.

---

3. Rev. 20:4
4. Rev. 20:5

Thus, they who come forth in the first resurrection shall *not* experience the second death. The rest, must suffer a thousand years before they can be redeemed, save for the beast and false prophet (and their type) who are destined to experience this second death forever and ever.

> 6 Blessed and holy is he that hath part in the first resurrection: on such the second death hath no power, but they shall be priests of God and of Christ, and shall reign with him a thousand years.[5]

After this thousand-year period is over, what did the angel declare would take place?

Satan shall be released from his prison to, once more, deceive and tempt the children of God. Eventually, wickedness shall permeate the world. Thus, John sees a repetition of history, as the armies of Satan, *again*, unite to battle the Lord. As this army prepares to annihilate the Saints, fire shall come down from heaven and destroy all his forces, only the Saints shall be left alive.

> 7 And when the thousand years are expired, Satan shall be loosed out of his prison,
> 8 And shall go out to deceive the nations which are in the four quarters of the earth, Gog and Magog, to gather them together to battle: the number of whom is as the sand of the sea.
> 9 And they went up on the breadth of the earth, and compassed the camp of the saints about, and the beloved city: and fire came down from God out of heaven, and devoured them.[6]

---

5. Rev. 20:6
6. Rev. 20:7-9

What will ultimately happen to Satan?

He shall join the beast and the false prophet, by being cast into the lake of fire and brimstone, where they shall be tormented day and night forever.

> *10 And the devil that deceived them was cast into the lake of fire and brimstone, where the beast and the false prophet are, and shall be tormented day and night for ever and ever.[7]*

Will Satan, the beast, and the false prophet, ever be able to return to where God the Father and Jesus Christ reside?

John is informed, that where God the Father reigns, there shall never be any place for them.

> *11 And I saw a great white throne, and him that sat on it, from whose face the earth and the heaven fled away; and there was found no place for them.[8]*

How will the final judgment take place?

All humanity must stand before God to receive their final judgment. At this time, the books shall be opened and all shall be judged from these books in accordance with their earthly works. Those who have accomplished much shall receive much, while they who have accomplished little shall receive little. After the last person is released from hell, then death and hell shall exist only for Satan and his co-conspirators as they continue to experience the second death.

---

7. Rev. 20:10
8. Rev. 20:11

12 And I saw the dead, small and great, stand before God; and the books were opened: and another book was opened, which is the book of life: and the dead were judged out of those things which were written in the books, according to their works.

13 And the sea gave up the dead which were in it; and death and hell delivered up the dead which were in them: and they were judged every man according to their works.

14 And death and hell were cast into the lake of fire. This is the second death.

15 And whosoever was not found written in the book of life was cast into the lake of fire.[9]

---

9. Rev. 20:12-15

21

The Holy City

The final judgment is complete. Each earthly participant has stood before the judgment bar of God. Some having heard the words, *"Depart from me, ye that work iniquity,"*[1] while others hear, *"Come, ye blessed of my Father, inherit the kingdom prepared for you from the foundation of the world:"*[2]

John is now carried away unto a high mountain, where he sees a holy city called the New Jerusalem, descending out of heaven, prepared as a bride adorned for her husband. The inhabitants of this city shall be they who have overcome the temptations of the adversary. This is the place where death, sorrow, and pain will be remembered no more. This is the place where liars, whoremongers, sorcerers, idolaters, and murderers shall not exist. This is the place where one is free to drink from the fountains of everlasting life. This is a place called *heaven,* a place of eternal happiness.

---

1. Matt. 7:23
2. Matt. 25:34

What will happen to our current heaven and earth?

Our current heaven and earth shall pass away and a new earth and a new heaven created.

> *1 And I saw a new heaven and a new earth: for the first heaven and the first earth were passed away; and there was no more sea.[3]*

As John looked, what did he see coming down from heaven?

He witnesses the descent of a glorious holy city, called New Jerusalem. This city is so beautiful that John said it was as a bride adorned for her husband.

> *2 And I John saw the holy city, new Jerusalem, coming down from God out of heaven, prepared as a bride adorned for her husband.[4]*

Who will dwell in this city?

A voice from heaven declared to John that God shall dwell with His people in this holy city.

> *3 And I heard a great voice out of heaven saying, Behold, the tabernacle of God is with men, and he will dwell with them, and they shall be his people, and God himself shall be with them, and be their God.[5]*

Will pain and sorrow exist any more for the inhabitants of this city?

---

3. Rev. 21:1
4. Rev. 21:2
5. Rev. 21:3

Death, sorrow, crying, and pain, John is told, shall no longer
be experienced; in other words, the conditions that caused so
much unhappiness during life on earth shall be gone forever.

> 4 And God shall wipe away all tears from their eyes; and
> there shall be no more death, neither sorrow, nor crying,
> neither shall there be any more pain: for the former things
> are passed away.[6]

Regarding the fountain of the water of life, what was promised?

Permission shall be given to drink from the fountain of the
water of life. In other words, the inhabitants of this city shall
be blessed with everlasting life. *"But whosoever drinketh of
the water that I shall give him shall never thirst; but the water
that I shall give him shall be in him a well of water springing
up into everlasting life."*[7]

> 5 And he that sat upon the throne said, Behold, I make all
> things new. And he said unto me, Write: for these words
> are true and faithful.
> 6 And he said unto me, It is done. I am Alpha and Omega,
> the beginning and the end. I will give unto him that is
> athirst of the fountain of the water of life freely.[8]

What other great blessings are in store for those who overcome the world?

Since they have overcome the trials and tribulations of earth
life, John now understands that they shall become co-inheritors
with Jesus Christ. In other words, He will be their God and they
shall be His sons.

6. Rev. 21:4
7. John 4:14
8. Rev. 21:5, 6

*7 He that overcometh shall inherit all things; and I will
be his God, and he shall be my son.*[9]

Will any of the followers of Satan be allowed into this city?

None of the unrighteous shall be allowed into this holy
place. The only thing Satan and his agents can expect to receive
is the second death.

*8 But the fearful, and unbelieving, and the abominable,
and murderers, and whoremongers, and sorcerers, and
idolaters, and all liars, shall have their part in the lake
which burneth with fire and brimstone: which is the second
death.*[10]

When one of the seven angels came to John, what did he show him?

Again, John is taken to a place where he can view the holy
Jerusalem descending out of heaven. With this vision, comes
more information about what this city represents and who shall
have access.

*9 And there came unto me one of the seven angels which
had the seven vials full of the seven last plagues, and talked
with me, saying, Come hither, I will shew thee the bride,
the Lamb's wife.*
*10 And he carried me away in the spirit to a great and
high mountain, and shewed me that great city, the holy
Jerusalem, descending out of heaven from God,*[11]

---

9. Rev. 21:7
10. Rev. 21:8
11. Rev. 21:9, 10

What is the glory of God?

The glory of God is manifest as a brilliant *light*. Since this city possesses the glory of God, it has the ability to emit a radiant *light*. This *light* is so beautiful the angel compared it to the reflection one might see from a jasper stone.

> *11 Having the glory of God: and her light was like unto a stone most precious, even like a jasper stone, clear as crystal;[12]*

Located along the city walls were twelve gates, guarded by twelve angels. What do these gates represent?

An angel explains to John that the twelve gates represent the twelve tribes of Israel.

> *12 And had a wall great and high, and had twelve gates, and at the gates twelve angels, and names written thereon, which are the names of the twelve tribes of the children of Israel:*
> *13 On the east three gates; on the north three gates; on the south three gates; and on the west three gates.[13]*

What does the foundation of the wall surrounding the city symbolize?

John sees that this city wall is built on twelve great foundations. Imbedded in each foundation is found the name of an apostle of the Lord, in honor of the apostles and prophets who form the foundation for the Church of Jesus Christ.

---

12. Rev. 21:11
13. Rev. 21:12, 13

14 And the wall of the city had twelve foundations, and in them the names of the twelve apostles of the Lamb.[14]

How large is the city, and how high are the walls, which surround it?

This city, explains the angel, is approximately 1400 miles in breadth, width, and height. In other words, it is a cube, and the walls are about 216 feet high.

15 And he that talked with me had a golden reed to measure the city, and the gates thereof, and the wall thereof.

16 And the city lieth foursquare, and the length is as large as the breadth: and he measured the city with the reed, twelve thousand furlongs. The length and the breadth and the height of it are equal.

17 And he measured the wall thereof, an hundred and forty and four cubits, according to the measure of a man, that is, of the angel.[15]

Why did the angel mention the gold and precious stones that were designed and built into the construction of this city?

Interestingly, many who joined with the whore of Babylon sold their souls to obtain great wealth; while the inhabitants of this holy city originally joined the Church of Jesus Christ *not* for wealth, but to serve God. However, in the end, by being obedient to the commandments of Christ, they not only magnified their character attributes and developed lasting ties to family and friends, but shall also enjoy great wealth and happiness.

---

14. Rev. 21:14
15. Rev. 21:15-17

18 And the building of the wall of it was of jasper: and the city was pure gold, like unto clear glass.

19 And the foundations of the wall of the city were garnished with all manner of precious stones. The first foundation was jasper; the second, sapphire; the third, a chalcedony; the fourth, an emerald;

20 The fifth, sardonyx; the sixth, sardius; the seventh, chrysolite; the eighth, beryl; the ninth, a topaz; the tenth, a chrysoprasus; the eleventh, a jacinth; the twelfth, an amethyst.

21 And the twelve gates were twelve pearls; every several gate was of one pearl: and the street of the city was pure gold, as it were transparent glass.[16]

Why is there no temple in this city?

John did not see a temple because the temple was only a facility to help carry out God's work to bring to pass the eternal life and exaltation of man. Since the individuals in this city have all achieved this reward, there is no need for a temple.

22 And I saw no temple therein: for the Lord God Almighty and the Lamb are the temple of it.[17]

Who else will bring their glory into this city?

The *light* the Lord emanates is so bright that it *lights* up the whole city. John sees that the people who inhabit this city are fortunate to be able to benefit from the Lord's great qualities. He also observes that those righteous individuals who have been rewarded with their own kingships shall bring their glory and honor into the city. Because of this *light*, there is no darkness in this city and therefore, no need to shut the gates.

---

16. Rev. 21:18-21
17. Rev. 21:22

23 And the city had no need of the sun, neither of the moon, to shine in it: for the glory of God did lighten it, and the Lamb is the light thereof.

24 And the nations of them which are saved shall walk in the light of it: and the kings of the earth do bring their glory and honour into it.

25 And the gates of it shall not be shut at all by day: for there shall be no night there.

26 And they shall bring the glory and honour of the nations into it.[18]

What is the one requirement each person must meet to live in this holy city?

Everyone must have his (or her) name written in the Lamb's book of life. Liars, hate mongers, blasphemers, and they who corrupt and defile shall never complete this requirement.

27 And there shall in no wise enter into it any thing that defileth, neither whatsoever worketh abomination, or maketh a lie: but they which are written in the Lamb's book of life.[19]

---

18. Rev. 21:23-26
19. Rev. 21:27

22

Blessings for the Righteous

After describing the construction and exquisite décor of the New Jerusalem, the angel is ready to show John some benefits of living in this holy city. John sees a tree of life that yields fruit for the healing of the nations and sustenance for eternal life. Individuals allowed to inhabit this city may partake from this tree, thus, ending the curse from eating the forbidden fruit that initially separated Adam and Eve from God. Individuals, who have obeyed the commandments of God, shall finally know the real meaning of the phrase: *Each man according to his works*. Individuals, who have overcome, shall now dwell in full society with God the Father and His Son Jesus Christ, as His beloved sons and daughters, with all the rights and privileges associated with this endowment.

What did John see, concerning a river of water and tree of life?

John beholds a pure river of water proceeding forth from the throne of God and Jesus Christ. This water flows down the middle of a wide street. On either side of this river is a tree, called *the tree of life*, which represents *the love of God* through the *Atonement* of Jesus Christ. *"For God so loved the world, that he gave his only begotten son, that whosoever believeth in him should not perish, but have everlasting life."*[1] This tree yields twelve types of fruit each month. Thus the fruit carries with it the power of everlasting life. The leaves of this tree are for the spiritual healing of the nations as they abstain from war by emulating the love God has for them in their dealings with each other.

> *1 And he shewed me a pure river of water of life, clear as crystal, proceeding out of the throne of God and of the Lamb.*
> *2 In the midst of the street of it, and on either side of the river, was there the tree of life, which bare twelve manner of fruits, and yielded her fruit every month: and the leaves of the tree were for the healing of the nations.*[2]

When the angel informed John that there shall be no more curse, what was the significance?

In the Garden of Eden, Adam and Eve were told by God that *if they partook from the forbidden tree they would not only die, but also the ground would be cursed so that in sorrow they would eat of it all the days of their lives.*[3] Now that the Saints have overcome, this curse is no longer in effect. All elements required for everlasting life and happiness shall be freely available. Moreover, God the Father and Jesus Christ shall have their thrones there, and as an expression of appreciation, the Saints shall want to serve the Father and the Lamb forever.

---

1. John 3:16
2. Rev. 22:1, 2
3. See Gen. 2:9, 17; 3:17-19, 24

3 And there shall be no more curse: but the throne of
God and of the Lamb shall be in it; and his servants shall
serve him:⁴

Whose face will they see?

The inhabitants of this city, the angel explains, shall see the
face of God, with whom they have been sealed unto eternal life
and exaltation.

4 And they shall see his face; and his name shall be in
their foreheads.⁵

What is the meaning of the words, "For the Lord God giveth them light"?

As both God the Father and Jesus Christ emit a glorious
light from their immortal bodies, God shall give those who reign
with him *light*. In other words, their immortal bodies shall also
emit a similar form of *light* that shall help illuminate this holy
city forever.

5 And there shall be no night there; and they need no
candle, neither light of the sun; for the Lord God giveth
them light: and they shall reign for ever and ever.⁶

How does the angel conclude his visit to John?

He signifies to the truthfulness of this vision by bearing a
final testimony that God did send him to show John those things,
which shall soon take place.

---

4. Rev. 22:3
5. Rev. 22:4
6. Rev. 22:5

6 And he said unto me, These sayings are faithful and true: and the Lord God of the holy prophets sent his angel to shew unto his servants the things which must shortly be done.[7]

What kind of encouragement does John receive?

The Savior shall come suddenly, the angel exclaimed. Moreover, blessed is he who shall respond to the warnings and the promises of this book.

7 Behold, I come quickly: blessed is he that keepeth the sayings of the prophecy of this book.[8]

How did John surprise the angel?

After seeing and hearing these things, John fell on his knees to worship his host. The angel gently chides John by saying; *he is only a fellow servant who keeps the teachings of this book.* In other words, John is advised that it is not appropriate to worship angels, we should only worship God.

8 And I John saw these things, and heard them. And when I had heard and seen, I fell down to worship before the feet of the angel which shewed me these things.
9 Then saith he unto me, See thou do it not: for I am thy fellowservant, and of thy brethren the prophets, and of them which keep the sayings of this book: worship God,[9]

Should the prophecies outlined in this book be kept secret?

---

7. Rev. 22:6
8. Rev. 22:7
9. Rev. 22:8, 9

On the contrary, John is tasked *not* to keep this information secret, for the time is at hand to give it to the world.

> *10 And he saith unto me, Seal not the sayings of the prophecy of this book: for the time is at hand.*[10]

As to the wicked who will never take the opportunity to repent, how will they be judged?

At the final judgment, those who are unjust shall still be unjust, those who are filthy shall still be filthy, those who are righteous shall still be righteous, and those who are holy shall still be holy.

> *11 He that is unjust, let him be unjust still: and he which is filthy, let him be filthy still: and he that is righteous, let him be righteous still: and he that is holy, let him be holy still.*[11]

What role does "works" play in the reward process?

The angel declares that the Savior shall come suddenly, and when He comes each person shall be judged according to his own works.

> *12 And, behold, I come quickly; and my reward is with me, to give every man according as his work shall be.*[12]

Why is it important to obey the commandments of God?

---

10. Rev. 22:10
11. Rev. 22:11
12. Rev. 22:12

Those who obey His commandments shall have access to the holy city and the tree of life; but the sorcerers, whoremongers, murderers, idolaters, and deceivers shall be left without.

> *13 I am Alpha and Omega, the beginning and the end, the first and the last.*
>
> *14 Blessed are they that do his commandments, that they may have right to the tree of life, and may enter in through the gates into the city.*
>
> *15 For without are dogs, and sorcerers, and whoremongers, and murderers, and idolaters, and whosoever loveth and maketh a lie.[13]*

According to the angel, what does Jesus want everyone to know?

He wants all to know that He has sent His angel to testify of these things, and that (in addition to His other names) He is known as the Morning Star.

> *16 I Jesus have sent mine angel to testify unto you these things in the churches. I am the root and the offspring of David, and the bright and morning star.[14]*

What else does the Lord want each person to comprehend?

He wants each of us to understand that His gospel is available for anyone who wants to drink of the water of everlasting life,[15] and experience the joy and happiness that comes from the love of God.

---

13. Rev. 22:13-15
14. Rev. 22:16
15. See John 4:14

*17 And the Spirit and the bride say, Come. And let him
that heareth say, Come. And let him that is athirst come.
And whosoever will, let him take the water of life freely.*[16]

If any person shall change or alter the words in the Book of Revelation, what will happen?

God shall give him the plagues of this book, then delete his
name from the book of life and deny him access to the holy city.

*18 For I testify unto every man that heareth the words
of the prophecy of this book, If any man shall add unto
these things, God shall add unto him the plagues that are
written in this book:
19 And if any man shall take away from the words of the
book of this prophecy, God shall take away his part out
of the book of life, and out of the holy city, and from the
things which are written in this book.*[17]

What are the final words of this book?

The Lord wants John to know that these words are true, that
He shall come suddenly, and that the grace of the Lord shall be
with all who read these words.

*20 He which testifieth these things saith, Surely I come
quickly. Amen. Even so, come, Lord Jesus.
21 The grace of our Lord Jesus Christ be with you all.
Amen.*[18]

While addressing the seven churches, many rewards were promised by the Lord for those who remain faithful. What are some of these blessings?

---

16. Rev. 22:17
17. Rev. 22:18, 19
18. Rev. 22:20, 21

Listed below are the blessings that are promised to those individuals who, at the final judgment hear the words, *"Come, ye blessed of my Father, inherit the kingdom prepared for you from the foundation of the world."*[19]

- They shall eat of the tree of life.[20]
- They shall receive a crown of life.[21]
- They shall not be hurt by the second death.[22]
- They shall eat of the hidden manna.[23]
- They shall be given a white stone.[24]
- They shall receive power over other nations.[25]
- They shall receive the morning star.[26]
- They shall be clothed in white raiment.[27]
- They shall have their name written in the book of life.[28]
- They shall hear Jesus Christ confess their name before God the Father.[29]
- They shall become a pillar in the temple of God.[30]
- They shall carry the name of God.[31]
- They shall inhabit the New Jerusalem.[32]
- They shall sit with Jesus in His throne.[33]

---

19. Matt. 25:34
20. Rev. 2:7
21. Rev. 2:10
22. Rev. 2:11
23. Rev. 2:17
24. Rev. 2:17
25. Rev. 2:26
26. Rev. 2:28
27. Rev. 3:5
28. Rev. 3:5
29. Rev. 3:5
30. Rev. 3:12
31. Rev. 3:12
32. Rev. 3:12
33. Rev. 3:21

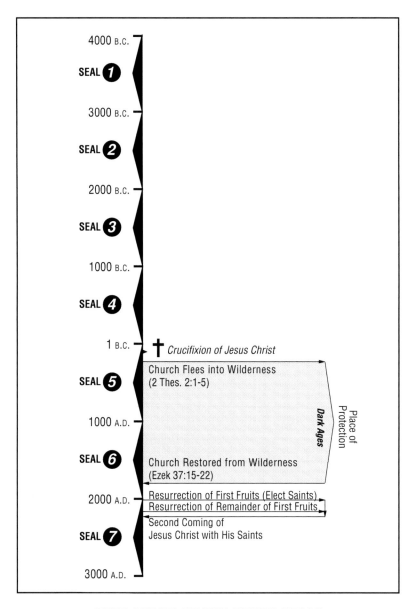

TIME CHART OF THE SEVEN SEALS

ILLUSTRATION A

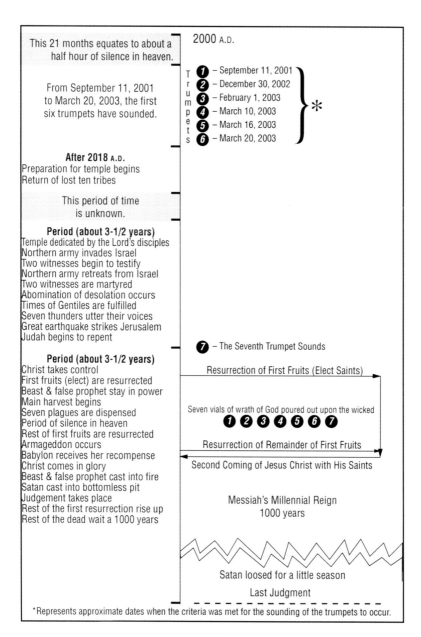

This 21 months equates to about a half hour of silence in heaven.

From September 11, 2001 to March 20, 2003, the first six trumpets have sounded.

2000 A.D.

T r u m p e t s

❶ – September 11, 2001
❷ – December 30, 2002
❸ – February 1, 2003
❹ – March 10, 2003
❺ – March 16, 2003
❻ – March 20, 2003
} *

After 2018 A.D.
Preparation for temple begins
Return of lost ten tribes

This period of time
is unknown.

Period (about 3-1/2 years)
Temple dedicated by the Lord's disciples
Northern army invades Israel
Two witnesses begin to testify
Northern army retreats from Israel
Two witnesses are martyred
Abomination of desolation occurs
Times of Gentiles are fulfilled
Seven thunders utter their voices
Great earthquake strikes Jerusalem
Judah begins to repent

❼ – The Seventh Trumpet Sounds

Period (about 3-1/2 years)
Christ takes control
First fruits (elect) are resurrected
Beast & false prophet stay in power
Main harvest begins
Seven plagues are dispensed
Period of silence in heaven
Rest of first fruits are resurrected
Armageddon occurs
Babylon receives her recompense
Christ comes in glory
Beast & false prophet cast into fire
Satan cast into bottomless pit
Judgement takes place
Rest of the first resurrection rise up
Rest of the dead wait a 1000 years

Resurrection of First Fruits (Elect Saints)

Seven vials of wrath of God poured out upon the wicked
❶ ❷ ❸ ❹ ❺ ❻ ❼

Resurrection of Remainder of First Fruits

Second Coming of Jesus Christ with His Saints

Messiah's Millennial Reign
1000 years

Satan loosed for a little season

Last Judgment

*Represents approximate dates when the criteria was met for the sounding of the trumpets to occur.

TIME CHART OF THE SEVEN TRUMPETS & SEVEN VIALS

ILLUSTRATION B

Part II

Reconciling *Revelation* with Mormon Prophecies

23

Prologue

15 Behold, when ye shall rend that veil of unbelief which doth cause you to remain in your awful state of wickedness, and hardness of heart, and blindness of mind, then shall the great and marvelous things which have been hid up from the foundation of the world from you—yea, when ye shall call upon the Father in my name, with a broken heart and a contrite spirit, then shall ye know that the Father hath remembered the covenant which he made unto your fathers, O house of Israel.

16 And then shall my revelations which I have caused to be written by my servant John be unfolded in the eyes of all the people. Remember, when ye see these things, ye shall know that the time is at hand that they shall be made manifest in very deed.[1]

Years ago, as I began to study prophecies from the Bible in conjunction with Mormon prophecies, I noticed that (in some cases) the prophecies seemed to contradict one another. For example, according to JST 1 Thessalonians 4:16-17, the Lord shall descend from heaven, and the dead who served Christ shall rise first; then those who are alive shall be caught up to meet the Lord in the air.

16 For the Lord himself shall descend from heaven with a

---

1. Ether 4:15, 16

> *shout, with the voice of the archangel, and with the trump*
> *of God: and the dead in Christ shall rise first:[2]*
> *17 Then they who are alive shall be caught up together in*
> *the clouds with them who remain, to meet the Lord in the*
> *air: and so shall we be ever with the Lord.[3]*

However, when discussing what seems to be the same event, The Doctrine and Covenents 88:96-97 appears to present the opposite sequence.

> *96 And the saints that are upon the earth, who are alive,*
> *shall be quickened and be caught up to meet him.[4]*
> *97 And they who have slept in their graves shall come*
> *forth, for their graves shall be opened; and they also*
> *shall be caught up to meet him in the midst of the pillar*
> *of heaven —[5]*

Another sequence issue occurs with Revelation 8:1-6. As the seventh seal is opened, John sees that there is silence in heaven for about half an hour. This period of half an hour marks the beginning of when the next seven angels prepare to sound their trumps. This act will cause great destruction to come upon the wicked.

> *1 And when he had opened the seventh seal, there was*
> *silence in heaven about the space of half an hour.[6]*
> *2 And I saw the seven angels which stood before God; and*
> *to them were given seven trumpets.[7]*
> *3 And another angel came and stood at the altar, having a*
> *golden censer; and there was given unto him much insense,*
> *that he should offer it with the prayers of all saints upon*
> *the golden altar which was before the throne.[8]*
> *4 And the smoke of the incense, which came with the*
> *prayers of the saints, ascended up before God out of the*
> *angel's hand.[9]*

---

2. 1 Thes, 4:16   6. Rev. 8:1   9. Rev. 8:4
3. JST 1 Thes, 4:17   7. Rev. 8:2
4. D&C 88:96   8. Rev. 8:3
5. D&C 88:97

*5 And the angel took the censer, and filled it with fire of
the altar, and cast it into the earth: and there were vioces,
and thunderings, and lightnings, and an earthquake.[10]
6 And the seven angels which had the seven trumpts
prepared themselves to sound.[11]*

However, The Doctrine and Covenents 88:95 appears to proclaim that when this half hour is finished, the curtain of heaven
will be unfolded, and the face of the Lord shall be revealed.

*95 And there shall be silence in heaven for the space of half
an hour; and immediately after shall the curtain of heaven
be unfolded, as a scroll is unfolded after it is rolled up,
and the face of the Lord shall be unveiled;[12]*

The resurrection presents another timing discrepancy. Most
Mormon scholars subscribe to the theory that, at the last days,
only one resurrection will take place, whereby, the elect and
first fruits of Christ will come forth in the morning of the first
resurrection and be caught up to meet the Lord as He comes to
earth on a white horse wearing crowns of victory on His head.

For example, one highly respected Mormon author taught:
"Those being resurrected with celestial bodies, whose destiny
is to inherit a celestial kingdom, will come forth in the morning
of the first resurrection. Their graves shall be opened and they
shall be caught up to meet the Lord at His Second Coming. They
are Christ's, the first fruits, and they shall descend with him to
reign as kings and priests during the millennial era."[13]

However, there is evidence from the book of Revelation and
other biblical scriptures that suggests that those celestial bodies,
whose destiny is to inherit a celestial kingdom, will be resurrected
in two completely separate events that will occur approximately
three and a half years (forty-two months) from each other.

---

10. Rev. 8:5
11. Rev. 8:6
12. D&C 88:95

13. D. & C. 29:13; 43:18; 76:50-70; 88:97-98;
1 Thess. 4:16-17; Rev. 20:3-7 (MORMON
DOCTRINE, Bruce R. McConkie, Second
Edition, Bookcraft, Salt Lake City, Utah p. 640)

Is there a solution to this dilemma? The short answer is yes! The primary purpose of this book is to show how the book of Revelation and Mormon prophecies reconcile these seemingly insurmountable contradictions into one beautiful picture.

A secondary purpose of Part II is to show that only a prophet of God, such as Joseph Smith Jr., or John the Revelator, could have been aware of this information because of the intriguing way it was woven together with other ancient holy scriptures to show how the events of the last days will play out.

As a young Cub Scout I can remember spending hours weaving together various strands of colored plastic strips into chains that could be attached to knives, eating utensils, or other scouting paraphernalia. In a way, the reconciliation procedure outlined in Part II is somewhat similar because it involves the weaving of three incomplete strands of scripture timelines together to form a complete, understandable, single, timeline event. These three incomplete strands of scripture timelines come from Section 88 of The Doctrine and Convents, Joseph Smith Translation of the last paragraph of Matthew 23, and all of Matthew 24, and the book of *Revelation*. A few strands of other scriptural references were also woven in to provide clarification and enhanced understanding as necessary. I also purposely used the three primary sources listed above because the information they provide came straight from the Lord, in such a way, as to avoid serious contamination.

In Alexander Pope's poem "Vice" he wrote:

> *Vice is a monster of so frightful mien,*
> *As to be hated needs but to be seen;*
> *Yet seen too oft, familiar with her face,*
> *We first endure, then pity, then embrace.*

This is exactly what has been happening over the last few years pertaining to the degradation of our moral society. Not too many years ago the actions of the decadent were conducted in the hidden seedy places of humanity. Today, because of the erosion of the moral fiber of our culture, these actions are carried out, not only in the light of day, but paraded before our senses in such a blatant way as if to say: "I dare you to try and stop me." It's as if society is on a roller coaster that is descending at an ever-increasing speed towards self-destruction. With this in mind, I have felt an increasing urgency that the public needs to be aware of what is happening. This is the reason for this book, it is simply a survival manual to help one overcome the events of the last days.

It should be noted that all efforts were made to be accurate and in accordance with the doctrines of The Church of Jesus Christ of Latter-day Saints; however, the author is solely responsible for the contents of this book.

Explainations Concerning Abbreviations:

JST . . . . . . Joseph Smith Translation
D&C . . . . . Doctrine and Covenants
HC. . . . . . . History of the Church by Joseph Smith
TPJS . . . . . Teachings of the Prophet Joseph Smith

24

Unlocking the Signs of the Times

To help prepare to implement the reconciliation process it is necessary to review some of the events that will transpire prior to the final arrival of Jesus Christ.

When will it become apparent that the coming of the Son of Man is near?

The Church of Jesus Christ of Latter-day Saints will construct a temple in Jerusalem. This is not the third temple that the Jews are expected to build upon their sacred temple mount; when that Jewish temple is erected, it will never be defiled. What evidence is available to confirm this assertion? When discussing potential sites of refuge that will be set up to protect His Saints, the Lord speaks of a place in Jerusalem. He identifies this location as where the Saints conduct baptisms for their dead.

> *36 For it is ordained that in Zion, and in her stakes, and in Jerusalem, those places which I have appointed for refuge,*

shall be the places for your baptisms for your dead.[1]

Currently, baptisms for the dead take place only within the confines of a Latter-day Saint temple.

What will be the next clue that the end of days, prophesied by the prophets, is fast approaching?

From the north countries, a special group from the lost ten tribes will appear. Currently, members of the lost ten tribes are being gathered from the far corners of the earth; however, there is a certain company of righteous Israelites that will be gathered in such a way as to leave no doubt that the end is near. Some scholars have suggested that this group will not arrive until after the Second Coming. However, there is evidence to suggest otherwise. For example, once the Second Coming occurs, all the wicked shall be removed from the face of the earth, yet, according to the Lord, as this special group travels toward Zion, its enemies shall become a prey unto it. If all the wicked are taken from the earth during the Second Coming, who will be their enemies?

> *26 And they who are in the north countries shall come in remembrance before the Lord; and their prophets shall hear his voice, and shall no longer stay themselves; and they shall smite the rocks, and the ice shall flow down at their presence.[2]*
> *27 And an highway shall be cast up in the midst of the great deep.[3]*
> *28 Their enemies shall become a prey unto them,[4]*
> *29 And in the barren deserts there shall come forth pools of living water; and the parched ground shall no longer be a thirsty land.[5]*

---

1. D&C 124:36   4. D&C 133:28
2. D&C 133:26   5. D&C 133:29
3. D&C 133:27

30 And they shall bring forth their rich treasures unto the children of Ephraim, my servants.[6]
31 And the boundaries of the everlasting hills shall tremble at their presence.[7]
32 And there shall they fall down and be crowned with glory, even in Zion, by the hands of the servants of the Lord, even the children of Ephraim,[8]

How will a certain last ditch effort be seen as a comforting sign that many souls will escape the wrath of God?

A last ditch effort for the gospel to be preached in all the world will occur, and then the end shall come.

31 And again, this Gospel of the Kingdom shall be preached in all the world, for a witness unto all nations, and then shall the end come, or the destruction of the wicked;[9]
84 Therefore, tarry ye, and labor diligently, that you may be perfected in your ministry to go forth among the Gentiles for the last time, as many as the mouth of the Lord shall name, to bind up the law and seal up the testimony, and to prepare the saints for the hour of judgment which is to come;[10]
85 That their souls may escape the wrath of God, the desolation of abomination which awaits the wicked, both in this world and in the world to come.[11]

What missionary force will have the honor to take the gospel to the Gentiles for the last time?

Twelve thousand righteous sons of God from each of the twelve tribes of Israel (save Dan) shall have this honor.

---

6. D&C 133:30   9. JST Matt. 1:31
7. D&C 133:31   10. D&C 88:84
8. D&C 133:32   11. D&C 88:85

1 And after these things I saw four angels standing on the four corners of the earth, holding the four winds of the earth, that the wind should not blow on the earth, nor on the sea, nor on any tree.[12]

2 And I saw another angel ascending from the east, having the seal of the living God: and he cried with a loud voice to the four angels, to whom it was given to hurt the earth and the sea,[13]

3 Saying, hurt not the earth, neither the sea, nor the trees, till we have sealed the servants of our God in their foreheads.[14]

4 And I heard the number of them which were sealed: and there were sealed an hundred and forty and four thousand of all the tribes of the children of Israel.[15]

5 Of the tribe of Judah were sealed twelve thousand. Of the tribe of Reuben were sealed twelve thousand. Of the tribe of Gad were sealed twelve thousand.[16]

6 Of the tribe of Aser were sealed twelve thousand. Of the tribe of Nepthalim were sealed twelve thousand. Of the tribe of Manasses were sealed twelve thousand.[17]

7 Of the tribe of Simeon were sealed twelve thousand. Of the tribe of Levi were sealed twelve thousand. Of the tribe of Issachar were sealed twelve thousand.[18]

8 Of the tribe of Zabulon were sealed twelve thousand. Of the tribe of Joseph were sealed twelve thousand. Of the tribe of Benjamin were sealed twelve thousand.[19]

Who are these 144,00 servants of God, and what is their mission?

They are high priests, ordained to administer the gospel to bring as many as will come into the church of the Firstborn (Jesus Christ).

---

12. Rev. 7:1
13. Rev. 7:2
14. Rev. 7:3
15. Rev. 7:4

16. Rev. 7:5
17. Rev. 7:6
18. Rev. 7:7
19. Rev. 7:8

Q. What are we to understand by sealing the one hundred and forty-four thousand, out of all the tribes of Israel – twelve thousand out of every tribe?
A. We are to understand that those who are sealed are high priests, ordained unto the holy order of God, to administer the everlasting gospel; for they are they who are ordained out of every nation, kindred, tongue, and people, by the angels to whom is given power over the nations of the earth, to bring as many as will come to the church of the Firstborn.[20]

What advice will the Lord impart to this group as they prepare to depart for this last ditch mission?

They are to take no thought of what they should say, but allow the Spirit of God the Father speak through them.

16 Behold, I send you forth as sheep in the midst of wolves: be ye therefore wise as serpents, and harmless as doves.[21]
17 But beware of men: for they will deliver you up to the councils, and they will scourge you in their synagogues;[22]
18 And ye shall be brought before governors and kings for my sake, for a testimony against them and the Gentiles.[23]
19 But when they deliver you up, take no thought how or what ye shall speak: for it shall be given you in that same hour what ye shall speak.[24]
20 For it is not ye that speak, but the Spirit of your Father which speaketh in you.[25]
21 And the brother shall deliver up the brother to death, and the father the child: and the children shall rise up against their parents, and cause them to be put to death.[26]
22 And ye shall be hated of all men for my name's sake: but he that endureth to the end shall be saved.[27]

Will they complete their mission before the Son of Man comes in glory?

20. D&C 77:11
21. Matt. 10:16
22. Matt. 10:17
23. Matt. 10:18
24. Matt. 10:19
25. Matt. 10:20
26. Matt. 10:21
27. Matt. 10:22

No! The Son of Man will come before they will have had the opportunity to proselyte in every city of Israel.

> *23 But when they persecute you in this city, flee ye into another: for verily I say unto you, Ye shall not have gone over the cities of Israel, till the Son of man be come.*[28]

In conjunction with this group, two individuals shall appear in Jerusalem. Who are these people and what is their mission?

John simply refers to these people as the two witnesses. They shall prophesy where Christ was crucified (Jerusalem), (see Revelation 11:8) for three and a half Biblical years (42 months) clothed in sackcloth.

> *3 And I will give power unto my two witnesses, and they shall prophesy a thousand two hundred and threescore days, clothed in sackcloth.*[29]
> *4 These are the two olive trees, and the two candlesticks standing before the God of the earth.*[30]

The Lord provided Joseph Smith with additional information concerning these two individuals.

> *Q. What is to be understood by the two witnesses, in the eleventh chapter of Revelation?*
> *A. They are two prophets that are to be raised up to the Jewish nation in the last days, at the time of the restoration, and to prophesy to the Jews after they are gathered and have built the city of Jerusalem in the land of their fathers.*[31]

---

28. Matt. 10:23
29. Rev. 11:3
30. Rev. 11:4
31. D&C 77:15

What will happen to these two witnesses?

Eventually, the beast who ascends out of the bottomless pit, will kill them, and their bodies shall lie in the streets of Jerusalem for three and a half days while their enemies send gifts one to another to celebrate their demise.

> *7 And when they shall have finished their testimony, the beast that ascendeth out of the bottomless pit shall make war against them, and shall overcome them, and kill them.*[32]
> *8 And their dead bodies shall lie in the street of the great city, which spiritually is called Sodom and Egypt, where also our Lord was crucified.*[33]
> *9 And they of the people and kindreds and tongues and nations shall see their dead bodies three days and an half, and shall not suffer their dead bodies to be put in graves.*[34]
> *10 And they that dwell upon the earth shall rejoice over them, and make merry, and shall send gifts one to another; because these two prophets tormented them that dwelt on the earth.*[35]

After the two winesses are killed, what will happen to their bodies?

Following this event, the bodies shall be taken up to heaven while their enemies witness their resurrection with great fear and trepidation.

> *11 And after three days and an half the Spirit of life from God entered into them, and they stood upon their feet; and great fear fell upon them which saw them.*[36]
> *12 And they heard a great voice from heaven saying unto them, Come up hither. And they ascended up to heaven in a cloud; and their enemies beheld them.*[37]

---

32. Rev. 11:7   35. Rev. 11:10
33. Rev. 11:8   36. Rev. 11:11
34. Rev. 11: 9   37. Rev. 11:12

What is the next clue indicating that the coming of the Son of Man is near?

The abomination of desolation, spoken of by Daniel the prophet, will take place in Jerusalem.

> *32 And again shall the abomination of desolation, spoken of by Daniel the prophet, be fulfilled.*[38]
> *20 And when ye shall see Jerusalem compassed with armies, then know that the desolation thereof is nigh.*[39]
> *12 When you, therefore, shall see the abomination of desolation, spoken of by Daniel the prophet, concerning the destruction of Jerusalem, then you shall stand in the holy place; whoso readeth let him understand.*[40]
> *13 Then let them who are in Judea flee into the mountains;*[41]
> *14 Let him who is on the housetop flee, and not return to take anything out of his house;*[42]
> *15 Neither let him who is in the field return back to take his clothes;*[43]
> *16 And woe unto them that are with child, and unto them that give suck in those days;*[44]
> *17 Therefore, pray ye the Lord that your flight be not in the winter, neither on the Sabbath day;*[45]
> *18 For then, in those days, shall be great tribulation on the Jews and upon the inhabitants of Jerusalem, such as was not before sent upon Israel, of God, since the beginning of their kingdom until this time; no, nor ever shall be sent again upon Israel.*[46]
> *19 All things which have befallen them are only the beginning of the sorrows which shall come upon them.*[47]
> *20 And except those days should be shortened, there should none of their flesh be saved; but for the elect's sake, according to the covenant, those days shall be shortened.*[48]

---

38. JST Matt. 1:32	42. JST Matt. 1:14	46. JST Matt. 1:18
39. Luke 21:20	43. JST Matt. 1:15	47. JST Matt. 1:19
40. JST Matt. 1:12	44. JST Matt. 1:16	48. JST Matt. 1:20
41. JST Matt. 1:13	45. JST Matt. 1:17	

What is this abomination of desolation, spoken of by Daniel, which must be fulfilled?

The holy temple constructed by The Church of Jesus Christ of Latter-day Saints shall be defiled, the daily sacrifice of labor curtailed, sacred rooms vandalized, and Satan's minion will sit in the temple as if he is God.

> *31 And arms shall stand on his part, and they shall pollute the sanctuary of strength, and shall take away the daily sacrifice, and they shall place the abomination that maketh desolate.[49]*
> *11 Yea, he magnified himself even to the prince of the host, and by him the daily sacrifice was taken away, and the place of his sanctuary was cast down.[50]*
> *12 And an host was given him against the daily sacrifice by reason of transgression, and it cast down the truth to the ground; and it practised, and prospered.[51]*
> *3 Let no man deceive you by any means: for that day shall not come, except there come a falling away first, and that man of sin be revealed, the son of perdition;[52]*
> *4 Who opposeth and exalteth himself above all that is called God, or that is worshipped; so that he as God sitteth in the temple of God, shewing himself that he is God.[53]*

The person who is sitting in the temple of God, as if he is God, is referred to as "that man of sin, or the wicked one." What must happen to Satan (mystery of iniquity) before that man of sin can be revealed?

Satan must be taken out of the way. This does not mean he will have not have any influence in the continuation of his efforts to tempt all mankind, but it simply means he will not be

---

49. Dan. 11:31
50 Dan. 8:11
51. Dan 8:12

52. 2 Thes. 2:3
53. 2 Thes. 2:4

allowed to alter (or slow down) the chain of events that must occur before the Son of Man can come in His glory.

> *6 And now ye know what withholdeth that he might be revealed in his time.*[54]
> *7 For the mystery of iniquity doth already work, and he it is who now worketh, and Christ suffereth him to work, until the time is fulfilled that he shall be taken out of the way.*[55]

After Satan (he that worketh) is taken out of the way and the wicked one is revealed, who will finally curtail the reign of this individual?

Jesus Christ will curtail the reign of Satan's minion (the wicked one) when He comes to earth as Kings of Kings and Lord of Lords.

> *8 And then shall that wicked one be revealed, whom the Lord shall consume with the spirit of his mouth, and shall destroy with the brightness of his coming:*[56]
> *9 Yea, the Lord, even Jesus, whose coming is not until after there cometh a falling away, by the working of Satan with all power and signs and lying wonders,*[57]

What will happen after the gospel is preached in all the world and the abomination of desolation has taken place?

The wrath of God will be dispensed upon the earth, which will consist of earthquakes, thunderings, lightnings, tempests, and the waves of the sea heaving beyond their bounds. This wrath will complete the second woe.

---

54. 2 Thes. 2:6
55. JST 2 Thes. 2:7
56. JST 2 Thes. 2:8
57. JST 2 Thes. 2:9

88 And after your testimony cometh wrath and indignation upon the people.[58]

89 For after your testimony cometh the testimony of earthquakes, that shall cause groanings in the midst of her, and men shall fall upon the ground and shall not be able to stand.[59]

90 And also cometh the testimony of the voice of thunderings, and the voice of lightnings, and the voice of tempests, and the voice of the waves of the sea heaving themselves beyond their bounds.[60]

91 And all things shall be in commotions; and surely, men's hearts shall fail them; for fear shall come upon all people.[61]

12 And I beheld when he had opened the sixth seal, and, lo, there was a great earthquake; and the sun became black as sackcloth of hair, and the moon became as blood;[62]

13 And the stars of heaven fell unto the earth, even as a fig tree casteth her untimely figs, when she is shaken of a mighty wind.[63]

14 And the heavens opened as a scroll is opened when it is rolled together; and every mountain and island was moved out of its place.[64]

15 And the kings of the earth, and the great men, and the rich men, and the chief captains, and the mighty men, and every bondman, and every free man, hid themselves in the dens and in the rocks of the mountains;[65]

16 And said to the mountains and rocks, Fall on us, and hide us from the face of him that sitteth on the throne, and from the wrath of the Lamb:[66]

17 For the great day of his wrath is come; and who shall be able to stand?[67]

13 And the same hour was there a great earthquake, and the tenth part of the city fell, and in the earthquake were slain of men seven thousand: and the remnant were affrighted, and gave glory to the God of heaven.[68]

14 The second woe is past; and, behold, the third woe cometh quickly.[69]

---

58. D&C 88:88
59. D&C 88:89
60. D&C 88:90
61. D&C 88:91
62. Rev. 6:12
63. Rev. 6:13
64. JST Rev, 6:14
65. Rev. 6:15
66. Rev. 6:16
67. Rev. 6:17
68. Rev. 11:13
69. Rev. 11:14

25

Christ Begins His Covert Reign

Why hat angel will sound to announce the arrival of the third woe? It will be the seventh angel. It is this angel who will announce that the Lord is initiating His covert reign in order to accomplish all that needs to be completed before he can come to earth in all His glory.

> 15 And the seventh angel sounded; and there were great voices in heaven, saying, The kingdoms of this world are become the kingdoms of our Lord, and of his Christ; and he shall reign for ever and ever.[1]

What will happen when Christ begins His covert reign?

He will judge the dead (to determine the order in which the dead will be resurrected), reward His prophets, Saints, and those who revere His name. Once this is accomplished, He will destroy those who are destroying the earth.

---

1. Rev. 11:15

> *18 And the nations were angry, and thy wrath is come, and the time of the dead, that they should be judged, and that thou shouldest give reward unto thy servants the prophets, and to the saints, and them that fear thy name, small and great; and shouldest destroy them which destroy the earth.[2]*

What will happen as the seventh angel begins to sound?

The mystery of God shall be finished.

> *7 But in the days of the voice of the seventh angel, when he shall begin to sound, the mystery of God should be finished, as he hath declared to his servants the prophets.[3]*

What is this mystery of God?

It is the process by which a person is changed in the twinkiling of an eye from mortality into an immortal being. In short, it describes the resurrection procedure.

> *51 Behold, I shew you a mystery; We shall not all sleep, but we shall all be changed,[4]*
> *52 In a moment, in the twinkling of an eye, at the sound of the trump: for the trumpet shall sound, and the dead shall be raised incorruptible, and we shall be changed.[5]*
> *53 For this corruptible must put on incorruption, and this mortal must put on immortality.[6]*
> *54 So when this corruptible shall have put on incorruption, and this mortal shall have put on immortality, then shall be brought to pass the saying that is written, Death is swallowed up in victory.[7]*

---

2. Rev. 11:18
3. Rev. 10:7
4. 1 Cor. 15:51

5. JST 1 Cor. 15:52
6. 1 Cor. 15:53
7. 1 Cor. 15:54

What will happen immediately after the tribulation of those days?

The sun will be darkened, moon bathed in blood, and the stars will appear to fall from the heavens.

> *33 And immediately after the tribulation of those days, the sun shall be darkened, and the moon shall not give her light, and the stars shall fall from heaven, and the powers of heaven shall be shaken.[8]*
>
> *87 For not many days hence and the earth shall tremble and reel to and fro as a drunken man; and the sun shall hide his face, and shall refuse to give light; and the moon shall be bathed in blood; and the stars shall become exceedingly angry, and shall cast themselves down as a fig that falleth from off a fig tree.[9]*

Just how important is this sign?

In February 1843, the Prophet Joseph read in a local newspaper that a man from Illinois had recently reported seeing the sign of the Second Coming early one morning. When the editor of the paper challenged the Prophet about this, Joseph sent his reply in a letter to the Church newspaper, he wrote: "Notwithstanding Mr. Redding may have seen a wonderful appearance in the clouds one morning about sunrise (which is nothing very uncommon in the winter season), he has not seen the sign of the Son of Man, as foretold by Jesus; neither has any man, nor will any man, until after the sun shall have been darkened and the moon bathed in blood."[10]

---

8. JST Matt. 1:33
9. D&C 88:87
10. HC 5:291

What will happen after the powers of the heavens are shaken, the sun appears darkened, and the moon is bathed in blood?

Then will appear the sign of the Son of Man in the heaven, and all those who are not prepared to meet the Lord at this time will mourn for their own safety.

> 36 And, as I said before, after the tribulation of those days, and the powers of the heavens shall be shaken, then shall appear the sign of the Son of Man in heaven, and then shall all the tribes of the earth mourn; and they shall see the Son of Man coming in the clouds of heaven, with power and great glory;[11]
> 92 And angels shall fly through the midst of heaven, crying with a loud voice, sounding the trump of God, saying: Prepare ye, prepare ye, O inhabitants of the earth; for the judgment of our God is come. Behold, and lo, the Bridegroom cometh; go ye out to meet him.[12]
> 93 And immediately there shall appear a great sign in heaven, and all people shall see it together.[13]

What is this great sign that shall appear in the heavens?

The sign is the coming of the Son of Man, which will be as the morning light coming out of the east. Apparently, the world will say it is a planet or comet. It appears that only those involved with this resurrection will be able see what is happening, much like when Stephen was the only one to witness God as he was being stoned to death.[14] Thus only their missing presence shall offer any clue as to what has just occurred. Though the world

---

11. JST Matt. 1:36
12. D&C 88:92
13. D&C 88:93
14. See Acts 6:8; 7:55-60

shall witness a strange brilliant light transiting from east to west, they will probably rationalize it as just a near miss from a passing celestial phenomenon.

> *Then will appear one grand sign of the Son of Man in heaven. But what will the world do? They will say it is a planet, a comet, etc, But the Son of Man will come as the sign of the coming of the Son of Man, which will be as a light of the morning cometh out of the east.*[15]

---

15. TPJS p. 287

26

The Resurrection of the Elect

Exactly who will be resurrected at this time? The Lord will gather His *elect* from the four winds, and from one end of heaven to the other.

> 37 And whoso treasureth up my word, shall not be deceived, for the Son of Man shall come, and he shall send his angels before him with the great sound of a trumpet, and they shall gather together the remainder of his elect from the four winds, from one end of heaven to the other.[1]

How, and in what order will the remainder of the elect be gathered?

As the Lord descends from heaven the dead in Christ shall rise first then those who are alive and remain shall be caught up to meet the Lord in the air.

---

1. JST Matt. 1:37

*16 For the Lord himself shall descend from heaven with a
shout, with the voice of the archangel, and with the trump
of God: and the dead in Christ shall rise first:[2]
17 Then they who are alive shall be caught up together in
to the clouds with them who remain, to meet the Lord in
the air: and so shall we be ever with the Lord.[3]
52 In a moment, in the twinkling of an eye, at the sound
of the trump: for the trumpet shall sound, and the dead
shall be raised incorruptible, and we shall be changed.[4]*

Will Joseph Smith be resurrected at this time?

Richard Skousen in his book, *His Return*,[5] provides some
interesting research concerning this subject: "Perhaps the most
thrilling news of the latter-day dispensation is the prophecy that
Joseph will return as a resurrected being to complete his work
here in mortality. Not only will he return, but he will be resurrected many years before the Second Coming so that he can
accomplish the various tasks that were specifically assigned to
him in the pre-mortal councils of God. References to Joseph's
resurrection and return can be found in the scriptures, in his own
teachings and in the discourses of several Church leaders..."

"One of those who learned of this magnificent doctrine
shortly after Joseph martyrdom was Parley P. Pratt. He was
on a mission in Wisconsin when he received the devastating
news that Joseph and Hyrum had been murdered at Carthage.
Shocked and stunned at the news, he immediately returned home
to Nauvoo, walking the last hundred miles from Peoria, Illinois
to Nauvoo. He was completely overwhelmed as to what advice
he should give the Saints when he arrived in Nauvoo. He later
describe the depth of his emotional turmoil:

---

2. 1 Thes. 4:16
3. JST 1 Thes. 4:17
4. JST 1 Cor. 15:52

5. *His Return* by Richard N.
Skousen, Verity Publishing, Inc.
Orem, Utah p. 83, 84, 85, 87, 88.

"I walked onward, weighted down as it were unto death,
When I could endure it no longer, I cried out aloud, saying,
'Oh, Lord, in the name of Jesus Christ I pray Thee, show
me what these things mean, and what I shall say to Thy
People?' "Suddenly the Spirit of God came upon me,
and filled my heart with joy and gladness indescribable;
and while the spirit of revelation glowed in my bosom
with a visible a warmth and gladness as it were fire, the
Spirit said unto me, 'Lift up your head and rejoice. For
behold, it is well with my servants Joseph and Hyrum. My
servant Joseph still holds the keys of my kingdom in this
dispensation, and he shall stand in due time on the earth,
in the flesh, and fulfill that to which he is appointed.[6]

"Parley was so astonished at this message (since it was a new doctrine to him) that he asked the Lord to repeat it, which He did. When Parley arrived in Nauvoo he told all of his friends of this delightful news, and he even taught it to the Saints in several Church meetings..."[7]

Though some could say that the Lord did not specifically say that Joseph would receive an early resurrection, that is not the impression that Parley understood. The knowledge he received left him so excited that he could hardly wait to see the Saints in Nauvoo to tell them the good news.

"Heber C. Kimball also poignantly described the future day when the Saints will return to Jackson County to build the city of New Jerusalem, and some of the stalwart brethren who will be there:

"I am pretty sure of one thing: we shall go to Jackson
County, Missouri; that is, those who do right and honor
their callings, doing what they have been told to do. You
will be blessed, and you will see the day when Presidents
Brigham Young, Heber C. Kimball, and Danies H.
Wells, and the twelve Apostles will be in Jackson County

---

6. Parley P. Pratt, Autobigraphy of Parley P. Pratt. (Salt Lake City: Deseret Book 1938, 1970) page 333
7. Autobiography of Parley P. Pratt. pp. 333-334

Missouri, laying out your inheritances. In the flesh? Of course. We should look well without being in the flesh! We shall be there in the flesh, and all our enemies' cannot prevent it. Brother Wells you may write that. You will be there, and Willard (Richards) will be there, and also Jedediah (M. Grant), and Joseph and Hyrum Smith, and David (W. Patten), and Parley (P. Pratt) and the day will be when I will see those men in the general assembly of the Church of the First Born, in the great council of God in Jerusalem, too. Will we want you to be along? I heard Joseph say twice that Brother Brigham and I should be in the council in Jerusalem, when there should be a uniting of the two divisions of God's government."[8]

The laying out of the city of Zion, or the New Jerusalem, will be accomplished prior to the Second Coming.

66 And it shall be called the New Jerusalem, a land of peace, a city of refuge, a place of safety for the saints of the Most High God;

67 And the glory of the Lord shall be there, and the terror of the Lord also shall be there, insomuch that the wicked will not come unto it, and it shall be called Zion.

68 And it shall come to pass among the wicked, that every man that will not take his sword against his neighbor must needs flee unto Zion for safety.

69 And there shall be gathered unto it out of every nation under heaven; and it shall be the only people that shall not be at war one with another.

70And it shall be said among the wicked: Let us not go up to battle against Zion, for the inhabitants of Zion are terrible: wherefore we cannot stand.[9]

---

8. Heber C. Kimball, April 7, 1861, Journal of Discourses 9:27
9. D & C 45:66-70

27

The Beast and the False Prophet are Revealed

What will happen after the remainder of the elect is resurrected? The woman (church) will fly into the wilderness where she can be protected from the serpent (Satan) for 42 months. In response, the dragon (Satan) will make war with the remnant of her seed (righteous followers of Christ) who keep the commandments of God.

> *13 And when the dragon saw that he was cast unto the earth, he persecuted the woman which brought forth the man child.[1]*
>
> *14 And to the woman were given two wings of a great eagle, that she might fly into the wilderness, into her place, where she is nourished for a time, and times, and half a time, from the face of the serpent.[2]*
>
> *15 And the serpent cast out of his mouth water as a flood after the woman, that he might cause her to be carried away of the flood.[3]*

1. Rev. 12:13
2. Rev. 12:14
3. Rev. 12:15

> *16 And the earth helped the woman, and the earth opened*
> *her mouth, and swallowed up the flood which the dragon*
> *cast out of his mouth.[4]*
> *17 And the dragon was wroth with the woman, and went*
> *to make war with the remnant of her seed, which keep the*
> *commandments of God, and have the testimony of Jesus*
> *Christ.[5]*

How will the dragon (Satan) make war with the remnant of her seed, who were not resurrected with the elect?

The dragon (Satan) will give the beast power, a seat, and authority to carry out a war against those who have a testimony of the Lord.

> *2 And the beast which I saw was like unto a leopard, and*
> *his feet were as the feet of a bear, and his mouth as the*
> *mouth of a lion: and the dragon gave him his power, and*
> *his seat, and great authority.[6]*

How will we recognize this beast when he receives his power, seat, and great authority from the dragon (Satan).

This beast will have a near career-ending disaster that will appear (at the time) to suggest that any future professional advancement is simply dead. However, this will not be the case, as the beast will rise like a phoenix to eventually rule the world.

> *3 And I saw one of his heads as it were wounded to death;*
> *and his deadly wound was healed: and all the world*
> *wondered after the beast.[7]*

---

4. Rev. 12:16
5. Rev. 12:17
6. Rev. 13:2
7. Rev. 13:3

> *4 And they worshipped the dragon which gave power unto the beast: and they worshipped the beast, saying, Who is like unto the beast? who is able to make war with him?*[8]

How long will this beast be able able to exercise the power he shall receive from Satan?

The beast (Satan's protégé) will be given power to continue for forty-two months in his effort to blaspheme God, His temple, and they who dwell in heaven.

> *5 And there was given unto him a mouth speaking great things and blasphemies; and power was given unto him to continue forty and two months.*[9]
> *6 And he opened his mouth in blasphemy against God, to blaspheme his name, and his tabernacle, and them that dwell in heaven.*[10]

What will the beast ultimately do with this power?

He will temporarily overcome the Saints and eventually shall rule over all kindreds, tongues, and nations.

> *7 And it was given unto him to make war with the saints, and to overcome them: and power was given him over all kindreds, and tongues, and nations.*[11]

Who will assist the first beast in helping him make war with the Saints?

Another beast, having two horns (two sources of power), is like a lamb (woman), and also speaks like a dragon (speaks with craftiness of Satan).

---

8. Rev. 13:4
9. Rev. 13:5
10. Rev. 13:6
11. Rev. 13:7

How could anyone think that this person is a woman? Long ago, when King David committed adultery with Bathsheba she became pregnant. To keep the world from discovering what really happened, David had Bathsheba's husband killed in battle. Later, the prophet Nathan chastised David and compared him to a thief who stole another person's lamb. Thus, Nathan compared the woman, Bathsheba, to a lamb.[12] One question does remain: Why would John use the term "he" when referring to this beast? It could be that the Lord did not want John to know the gender of the beast. Thus, when John saw the beast, he simply assumed it was a "he."

> *11 And I beheld another beast coming up out of the earth; and he had two horns like a lamb, and he spake as a dragon.[13]*

How much power will this second beast possess?

The second beast will exercise all the power of the first beast, including making fire come down from heaven to earth in the sight of men.

> *12 And he exerciseth all the power of the first beast before him, and causeth the earth and them which dwell therein to worship the first beast, whose deadly wound was healed.[14]*
> *13 And he doeth great wonders, so that he maketh fire come down from heaven on the earth in the sight of men,[15]*

What will this second beast do to all who dwell on the earth?

---

12. See 2 Sam. 12:1-10
13. Rev. 13:11
14. Rev. 13:12
15. Rev. 13:13

By performing such miracles, this second beast will deceive all who dwell on the earth into making of an image to the first beast.

> *14 And deciveth them that dwell on the earth by the means of those miracles which he had power to do in the sight of the beast; saying to them that dwell on the earth, that they should make an image to the beast, which had the wound by a sword, and did live.*[16]

How will this second beast make war with the Saints who will not worship the image of the first beast?

This *image* will possess the ability to collect information and pass this information along to others who will have the power to kill those who will not worship the image of the beast.

> *15 And he had power to give life unto the image of the beast, that the image of the beast should both speak, and cause that as many as would not worship the image of the beast should be killed.*[17]

How (specifically) can the image cause the death of someone who will not worship the first beast?

This image will possess the capability to record the names of all who pledge their allegiance to the beast by receiving a mark in their right hand or forehead in order to buy and sell. Those who will not take on this mark shall be considered disloyal and the penalty for not being willing to worship the beast will be death.

---

16. Rev. 13:14
17. Rev. 13:15

> *16 And he causeth all, both small and great, rich and poor, free and bond, to receive a mark in their right hand, or in their foreheads:*[18]
> *17 And that no man might buy or sell, save he that had the mark, or the name of the beast, or the number of his name.*[19]

Do the scriptures provide any more information concerning the identity of this second beast?

The second beast is also referred to in *Revelation* as a false prophet.

> *13 And I saw three unclean spirits like frogs come out of the mouth of the dragon, and out of the mouth of the beast, and out of the mouth of the false prophet.*[20]

Will the first beast receive help from any source other than the false prophet, and if so, how long with this union last?

The first beast will receive power and strength from ten kings that will help him establish his rule over the world. Since the ten kings will receive power as kings for one hour with the beast, and the beast will be given forty-two months to make war with the Lamb, it stands to reason that one-hour equals forty-two months. Thus, this is how long the beast and ten kings will work together to make war against the Lord and His Saints. When the one hour, or forty-two months has expired the Lamb will overcome the adversary, beast, false prophet, and ten kings to reign as King of kings and Lord of lords.

---

18. Rev. 13:16
19. Rev. 13:17
20. Rev. 16:13

12 And the ten horns which thou sawest are ten kings, which have received no kingdom as yet; but receive power as kings one hour with the beast.[21]
13 These have one mind, and shall give their power and strength unto the beast.[22]
5 And there was given unto him a mouth speaking great things and blastphemies; and power was given unto him to continue forty and two months.[23]
14 These shall make war with the Lamb, and the Lamb shall overcome them: for he is Lord of lords, and King of kings: and they that are with him are called, and chosen, and faithful.[24]

As the beast and false prophet are preparing to make war with the Lamb (Christ) and His followers, what will the Lord do to protect the remnant of His Saints who were not resurrected with the elect?

The Lord will establish safe areas in mount Zion (new Jerusalem), her stakes, and in old Jerusalem, as cities of refuge where the Saints and righteous pacifist can be protected from the wicked.

32 And it shall come to pass, that whosoever shall call on the name of the Lord shall be delivered: for in mount Zion and in Jerusalem shall be deliverance as the Lord hath said, and in the remnant whom the Lord shall call.[25]
36 For it is ordained that in Zion, and in her stakes, and in Jerusalem, those places which I have appointed for refuge, shall be the places for your baptisms for your dead.[26]
66 And it shall be called the new Jerusalem a land of peace, a city of refuge, a place of safety for the saints of the Most High God;[27]
67 And the glory of the Lord shall be there, and the terror of the Lord also shall be there, insomuch that the wicked will not come unto it, and it shall be called Zion.[28]

21. Rev. 17:12
22. Rev. 17:13
23. Rev. 13:5
24. Rev. 17:14

25. Joel 2:32
26. D&C 124:36
27. D&C 45:66
28. D&C 45:67

68 And it shall come to pass among the wicked, that every man that will not take his sword against his neighbor must needs flee unto Zion for safety.[29]

69 And there shall be gathered unto it out of every nation under heaven; and it shall be the only people that shall not be at war one with another.[30]

70 And it shall be said among the wicked: Let us not go up to battle against Zion, for the inhabitants of Zion are terrible; wherefore we cannot stand.[31]

71 And it shall come to pass that the righteous shall be gathered out from among all nations, and shall come to Zion, singing with songs of everlasting joy.[32]

23 The Lord's scourge shall pass over by night and by day, and the report thereof shall vex all people; yea, it shall not be stayed until the Lord come;[33]

24 For the indignation of the Lord is kindled against their abominations and all their wicked works.[34]

25 Nevertheless, Zion shall escape if she observe to do all things whatsoever I have commanded her.[35]

At this point, John is informed that a great Babylonian city shall fall. This is unusual because this prediction is too soon to be associated with the Babylonian destruction that shall occur just prior to the Second Coming. So what city could it possibly be?

As mentioned in chapter 14, it will be the city of New York (in the United States of America). In addition to the rationale previously provided, is there any supporting evidence to suggest that Joseph Smith, or any other Mormon prophets have expressed a similar opinion?

In the book, *His Return*, Richard N. Skousen reported an interesting occurrence.[36] "The Prophet Joseph had the opportunity to visit New York City in October 1832 when he and his

---

29. D&C 45:68
30. D&C 45:69
31. D&C 45:70
32. D&C 45:71

33. D&C 97:23
34. D&C 97:24
35. D&C 97:25
36. *His Return*, Skousen pp. 172, 173, 174

brethren were commanded by the Lord to go on a mission to preach to the people in Boston, Albany and New York City.... Years later Emmeline B. Wells ... commented in the *Relief Society Magazine* about this mission to New York City by the Prophet Joseph Smith and Bishop Newel K. Whitney. Bishop Whitney told her of a singular experience that occurred while they were there. She said,

> *"They were in the city of New York, staying at a hotel. They were staying on the third floor—that was as high as the houses were in New York at that time. Newel K. Whitney with the Prophet looked over unto Long Island Sound and the ocean, and he said to Newel K. Whitney, 'This city will yet be destroyed. There will not be one stone left upon another to tell where it stood.'"[37] ...*

"Wilford Woodruff also prophesied of the destruction of the wicked cities in the United States, and he described how it will occur. In 1863, President Young and the brethren had visited the Saints in Logan. When Wilford Woodruff arose to speak , he addressed his comments to the youth in attendance. ...He then said that they would remember this day in which the brethren had visited them:

> *"You will say; 'That was in the days when Presidents [Ezra T.] Benson and [Peter] Maughan presided over us; that was before New York was destroyed by an earthquake; it was before Boston was swept into the sea, by the sea heaving itself beyond its bounds; it was before Albany was destroyed by fire.'' President Young followed and said: "What Brother Woodruff has said is revelation and will be fulfilled."[38]*

---

37. Emmeline B. Wells, Relief Society Magazine, (October 1920) 7:10:563
38. Deseret News (November 12, 1884) 33:678

When the time arrives to decide whether, or not, to take the mark of the beast, what warning does the Lord want all to know?

Any person who receives the mark (as a pledge of loyalty to the beast), in order to buy and sell, will be subject to the wrath of God when the time comes for His fury to be poured out upon the wicked, and they will regret their decision for the rest of eternity.

> 9 And the third angel followed them, saying with a loud voice, If any man worship the beast and his image, and receive his mark in his forehead, or in his hand,[39]
> 10 The same shall drink of the wine of the wrath of God, which is poured out without mixture into the cup of his indignation; and he shall be tormented with fire and brimstone in the presence of the holy angels, and in the presence of the Lamb:[40]
> 11 And the smoke of their torment ascendeth up for ever and ever: and they have no rest day nor night, who worship the beast and his image, and whosoever receiveth the mark of his name.[41]

What major test must the Saints surmount while waiting for the Lord to intervene?

The righteous are simply to trust the Lord, exhibit patience, and keep the commandments of God. As the Lord has been patient with us, we must be patient and allow Him to accomplish all He needs to do before He can come in glory to reward His disciples.

> 12 Here is the patience of the saints: here are they that keep the commandments of God, and the faith of Jesus.[42]

---

39. Rev. 14:9
40. Rev. 14:10
41. Rev. 14:11
42. Rev. 14:12

***If a righteous person loses his, or her, physical life
in the approaching battle against the beast and false
prophet, what words of comfort does the Lord want
His disciples to know?***

When the hour of temptation shall come upon all the world,
as to whether or not, to take on the mark of the beast, many of
the righteous can expect to forfeit their lives, due to their refusal
to conform. To comfort those individuals, the Lord wants all His
disciples to know that blessed are the dead who die in the Lord
from henceforth, and to know that their works will follow them.

> *13 And I heard a voice from heaven saying unto me, Write,
> Blessed are the dead which die in the Lord from henceforth:
> Yea, saith the Spirit, that they may rest from their labours;
> and their works do follow them.[43]*

---

43. Rev. 14:13

28

The Harvest of the Wheat

E ventually, the beast and false prophet will have the world divided into two camps: those who have taken the mark of the beast versus those who have not. What will happen next? The Son of Man (Jesus Christ) will thrust in His sickle (as the signal) to initiate the reaping of the harvest of wheat (righteous) from the earth.

> *14 And I looked, and behold a white cloud, and upon the cloud one sat like unto the Son of man, having on his head a golden crown, and in his hand a sharp sickle.[1]*
> *15 And another angel came out of the temple, crying with a loud voice to him that sat on the cloud, Thrust in thy sickle, and reap: for the time is come for thee to reap; for the harvest of the earth is ripe.[2]*
> *16 And he that sat on the cloud thrust in his sickle on the earth; and the earth was reaped.[3]*

1. Rev. 14:14
2. Rev. 14:15
3. Rev. 14:16

After the Son of Man thrust in His sickle, what will happen on earth?

The beast and false prophet will accomplish the harvest of the wheat by carrying out their threat to annihilate those who will not take on the mark of the beast, in order to buy and sell. This will be the time when the early Christians, who were slain for the word of Christ, shall receive the answer to their long-awaited question: "How long O Lord before you avenge our blood on them who dwell on the earth?" This harvest will mark the fulfillment of the Lord's response when He said, that they should rest until the prophecy is fulfilled that their fellowservants and brethren, should be killed as they were.

> 9 And when he had opened the fifth seal, I saw under the altar the souls of them that were slain for the word of God, and for the testimony which they held:[4]
> 10 And they cried with a loud voice, saying, How long, O Lord, holy and true, dost thou not judge and avenge our blood on them that dwell on the earth?[5]
> 11 And white robes were given unto every one of them; and it was said unto them, that they should rest yet for a little season, until their fellowservants also and their brethren, that should be killed as they were, should be fulfilled.[6]

---

4. Rev. 6:9
5. Rev. 6:10
6. Rev. 6:11

29

The Harvest of the Grapes

What will happen to those individuals who unite with the beast by taking upon them his mark? They will be subjected to the harvest of the grapes, which shall be gathered and cast into the great winepress of the wrath of God. These are they who will come to know the angel who has power over fire, as the wicked receive their just reward when the burning takes place.

> *17 And another angel came out of the temple which is in heaven, he also having a sharp sickle.[1]*
>
> *18 And another angel came out from the altar, which had power over fire; and cried with a loud cry to him that had the sharp sickle, saying, Thrust in thy sharp sickle, and gather the clusters of the vine of the earth; for her grapes are fully ripe.[2]*
>
> *19 And the angel thrust in his sickle into the earth, and gathered the vine of the earth, and cast it into the great winepress of the wrath of God.[3]*
>
> *20 And the winepress was trodden without the city, and blood came out of the winepress, even unto the horse bridles, by the space of a thousand and six hundred furlongs.[4]*

---

1. Rev. 14:17
2. Rev. 14:18
3. Rev. 14:19
4. Rev. 14:20

How will the harvest of the grapes (wicked) occur?

Five angels will pour out their vials of wrath upon the earth. Resulting in grievous sores, toxification of water supplies, scorching heat, and depressing darkness, all of which will cause the wicked to gnaw their tongues for pain. Each plague is designed to reward the wicked with the same type of suffering they heaped upon the disciples of Christ.

> *1 And I heard a great voice out of the temple saying to the seven angels, Go your ways, and pour out the vials of the wrath of God upon the earth.[5]*
>
> *2 And the first went, and poured out his vial upon the earth; and there fell a noisome and grievous sore upon the men which had the mark of the beast, and upon them which worshipped his image.[6]*
>
> *3 And the second angel poured out his vial upon the sea; and it became as the blood of a dead man: and every living soul died in the sea.[7]*
>
> *4 And the third angel poured out his vial upon the rivers and fountains of waters; and they became blood.[8]*
>
> *5 And I heard the angel of the waters say, Thou art righteous, O Lord, which art, and wast, and shalt be, because thou hast judged thus.[9]*
>
> *6 For they have shed the blood of saints and prophets, and thou hast given them blood to drink; for they are worthy.[10]*
>
> *7 And I heard another out of the altar say, Even so, Lord God Almighty, true and righteous are thy judgments.[11]*
>
> *8 And the fourth angel poured out his vial upon the sun; and power was given unto him to scorch men with fire.[12]*
>
> *9 And men were scorched with great heat, and blasphemed the name of God, which hath power over these plagues: and they repented not to give him glory.[13]*
>
> *10 And the fifth angel poured out his vial upon the seat of the beast; and his kingdom was full of darkness; and they gnawed their tongues for pain,[14]*

---

5. Rev. 16:1   9. Rev. 16:5   13. Rev. 16:9
6. Rev. 16:2   10. Rev. 16:6   14. Rev. 16:10
7. Rev. 16:3   11. Rev. 16:7
8. Rev. 16:4   12. Rev. 16:8

*11 And blasphemed the God of heaven because of their
pains and their sores, and repented not of their deeds.*[15]

Knowing that the beast, false prophet, and ten kings are seething with anger because of the pain and suffering of what they are experiencing, what shall the Lord do that will allow the armies of the wicked to convene in one area where they can all be simultaniously destroyed?

When the sixth angel pours his vial, the Lord will dry up
the river Euphrates thereby opening the way where the dragon,
(Satan), beast and false prophet can entice the armies of the
world to gather at Armageddon.

*12 And the sixth angel poured out his vial upon the great
river Euphrates; and the water thereof was dried up, that
the way of the kings of the east might be prepared.*[16]
*13 And I saw three unclean spirits like frogs come out of
the mouth of the dragon, and out of the mouth of the beast,
and out of the mouth of the false prophet.*[17]
*14 For they are the spirits of devils, working miracles
which go forth unto the kings of the earth and of the whole
world, to gather them to the battle of that great day of
God Almighty.*[18]

Just before the battle of Armageddon begins, the Lord will alert the Saints that something extremely important is about to happen. What is this important event?

When the armies of the world are gathered to Armageddon,
the Lord shall alert His disciples that He will soon come as a thief

---

15. Rev. 16:11
16. Rev. 16:12
17. Rev. 16:13
18. Rev. 16:14

in the night, and that they are to remain faithful and maintain their watch so as not to miss the opportunity that will shortly arrive.

> *15 Behold, I come as a thief. Blessed is he that watcheth, and keepeth his garments, lest he walk naked, and they see his shame.*[19]
> *16 And he gathered them together into a place called in the Hebrew tongue Armagedden.*[20]

At this time, what will be the status of the church of Satan (Babylon)?

It will be bound in bundles, which no man can loose and ready to be burned.

> *94 And another angel shall sound his trump, saying: That great church, the mother of abominations, that made all nations drink of the wine of the wrath of her fornication, that persecuteth the saints of God, that shed their blood— she who sitteth upon many waters, and upon the islands of the sea—behold, she is the tares of the earth; she is bound in bundles; her bands are made strong, no man can loose them; therefore, she is ready to be burned. And he shall sound his trump both long and loud, and all nations shall hear it.*[21]

So what great city, which reigns over the kings of the earth, will symbolize the woman (church of Satan) during the last days?

As indicated in chapter 17, it will be Rome (the eternal city of Italy) located just of the coast of the Mediterranean Sea.

Concerning the city of Babylon, Bruce R. McConkie record-

---

19. Rev. 16:15
20. Rev. 16:16
21. D&C 88:94

ed, "The city is Rome; but she too is only a type and a figure. The city is all the cities of the world—San Francisco, Chicago, and New York City; London, Paris, and Berlin; Moscow, Tokyo, and Sao Paulo—all of which are subject to the rule and dominion of evil and carnality?"[22]

While it is true that the city of Babylon is a composite of all the great cities of the world that have allowed the adversary free reign, there is still only one city that stands out in history as being drunk with the blood of the Saints and martyrs of Jesus Christ. Thus, when the time comes for the symbol of the whore to be burned, Rome is the symbol that shall receive special attention, and then the rest of the cities that comprise the church of Satan shall receive their just reward.

> 5 And upon her forehead was a name written, MYSTERY, BABYLON THE GREAT, THE MOTHER OF HARLOTS AND ABOMINATIONS OF THE EARTH.[23]
>
> 6 And I saw the woman drunken with the blood of the saints, and with the blood of the martyrs of Jesus: and when I saw her, I wondered with great admiration.[24]
>
> 18 And the woman which thou sawest is that great city, which reigneth over the kings of the earth.[25]
>
> 8 And there followed another angel, saying, Babylon is fallen, is fallen, that great city, because she made all nations drink of the wine of the wrath of her fornication.[26]

---

22. McConkie, Millennial Messiah, 445
23. Rev. 17:5
24. Rev. 17:6
25. Rev. 17:18
26. Rev. 14:8

30

The Resurrection of the First Fruits

W hat will happen next? There will be silence in heaven for the space of half and hour; and then the curtain of heaven will be unfolded and the face of the Lord shall be unveiled.

95 And there shall be silence in heaven for the space of half an hour; and immediately after shall the curtain of heaven be unfolded, as a scroll is unfolded after it is rolled up, and the face of the Lord shall be unveiled;[1]

How will these Saints be resurrected, and in what order will they come forth?

The Saints that are upon the earth, who are alive, shall be resurrected and caught up to meet the Lord in the air. Then the dead shall come forth to meet the Lord in the midst of the pillar of heaven. Notice that the order in which the first fruits will come forth will be reversed. During the resurrection of the elect, the dead in Christ were the first to rise and then the living in Christ

---

1. D&C 88:95

were taken. During this resurrection, those who are alive will rise first, then those who are dead will be taken.

> 96 And the saints that are upon the earth, who are alive, shall be quickened and be caught up to meet him.[2]
> 97 And they who have slept in their graves shall come forth, for their graves shall be opened; and they also shall be caught up to meet him in the midst of the pillar of heaven—[3]

What is the name of the group who will comprise the elements of this resurrection?

Christ refers to this group as the *first fruits*. These are the remnant of righteous Saints who will overcome Satan and his minions by not taking the mark of the beast and enduring to the end. After being caught up to meet the Lord in the air, they will then descend with Him at His final coming.

> 98 They are Christ's, the first fruits, they who shall descend with him first, and they who are on the earth and in their graves, who are first caught up to meet him; and all this by the voice of the sounding of the trump of the angel of God.[4]

Do we know exactly when this resurrection will take place?

Concerning the day and the hour, no mortal man knows; however, as these events unfold over the years, the righteous, who are cognizant of the signs of the times, will not be surprised when Christ appears to reward His disciples.

---

2. D&C 88:96
3. D&C 88:97
4. D&C 88:98

40 But of that day, and hour, no one noweth; no, not the angels of God in heaven, but my Father only.[5]

What will the wicked be doing just before the Son of Man comes in His glory?

They will be buying, selling, eating, drinking, and marrying until the final burning occurs and all the wicked are destroyed.

> *41 But as it was in the days of Noah, so it shall be also at the coming of the Son of Man;*[6]
> *42 For it shall be with them, as it was in the days which were before the flood; for until the day that Noah entered into the ark they were eating and drinking, marrying and giving in marriage;*[7]
> *43 And knew not until the flood came, and took them all away; so shall also the coming of the Son of Man be.*[8]
> *26 And as it was in the days of Noe, so shall it be also in the days of the Son of man.*[9]
> *27 They did eat, they drank, they married wives, they were given in marriage, until the day that Noe entered into the ark, and the flood came, and destroyed them all.*[10]
> *28 Likewise also as it was in the days of Lot; they did eat, they drank, they bought, they sold, they planted, they builded;*[11]
> *29 But the same day that Lot went out of Sodom it rained fire and brimstone from heaven, and destroyed them all.*[12]

What warning is given to the righteous concerning this resurrection of the first fruits?

Be ready, do not delay, and when the time comes to depart Jerusalem do not give in to the urge to look back, but continue forward with trust in the Lord that all will be well.

---

5. JST Matt. 1:40   8. JST Matt. 1:43   11. Luke 17:28
6. JST Matt. 1:41   9. Luke 17:26   12. Luke 17:29
7. JST Matt. 1:42   10. Luke 17:27

31 In that day, the disciple who shall be on the housetop, and his stuff in the house, let him not come down to take it away: and he who is in the field, let him likewise not return back.[13]
32 Remember Lots wife.[14]
33 Whosoever shall seek to save his life shall lose it; and whosoever shall lose his life shall preserve it.[15]
34 I tell you, in that night there shall be two in one bed; the one shall be taken, and the other shall be left.[16]
35 Two shall be grinding together; the one shall be taken, and the other left.[17]
36 Two shall be in the field; the one shall be taken, and the other left.[18]

Where will these individuals be taken?

They will be gathered by the angels to where the resurrected body of Saints are awaiting together to join with the Lord as He comes in glory on a white horse wearing crowns of victory upon His head.

37 And they answered and said unto him, Where, Lord shall they be taken? And he said unto them, Wheresoever the body is gathered; or, in other words, whitheresoever the saints are gathered, thither will the eagles be gathered together, or thither will the remainder be gathered together. This he spake signifying the gathering of his saints; and of angels descending and gathering the remainder unto them; the one from the bed, the other from the grinding, and the other from the field, whithersoever he listeth. For verily there shall be new heavens and a new earth, wherein dwelleth righteousness. And there shall be no unclean thing; for the earth becoming old, even as a garment, having waxed in corruption, wherefore it vanisheth away, and the footstool remaineth sanctified, cleansed from all sin.[19]

---

13. JST Luke 17:31
14. Luke 17:32
15. Luke 17:33
16. JST Luke 17:34

17. JST Luke 17:35
18. JST Luke 17:36
19. JST Luke 17:37

*44 Then shall be fulfilled that which is written, that in the
last days, two shall be in the field, the one shall be taken,
and the other left;*[20]
*45 Two shall be grinding at the mill, the one shall be
taken, and the other left;*[21]

What will happen to the wicked who are left behind?

Feelings of anquish, dispair and heartache will permeate
the hearts of those who joined with Satan, the beast, and false
prophet. Thoughts of, "how could I have been so duped into
joining with and worshipping this trio of evil personalities?"
will fill the air. But dreadful decisions have been made that will
impact one's life for all eternity and now the time has arrived to
experience the wrath of God. At this moment, fire will rain from
heaven and the wicked will inherit their just reward.

*29 But the same day that Lot went out of Sodom it rained
fire and brimstone from heaven, and destroyed them all.*[22]
*30 Even thus shall it be in the day when the Son of man
is revealed.*[23]

What final words of advice does the Lord want His disciples to know?

To all men, watch and be ready for such an hour that you
think not, the Son of Man cometh.

*46 And what I say unto one, I say unto all men; watch,
therefore, for you know not at what hour your Lord doth
come.*[24]

---

20. JST Matt. 1:44   23. Luke 17:30
21. JST Matt. 1:45   24. JST Matt. 1:46
22. Luke 17:29

47 But know this, if the good man of the house had known in what watch the thief would come, he would have watched, and would not have suffered his house to have been broken up, but would have been ready.[25]

48 Therefore be ye also ready, for in such an hour as ye think not, the Son of Man cometh.[26]

---

25. JST Matt. 1:47
26. JST Matt. 1:48

31

Summary

L et us now examine the differences between the events surrounding *The Resurrection of the Remnant of the Elect and The Resurrection of the Remnant of the First Fruits*. We will accomplish this by doing a side-by-side comparison analysis to show how these two resurrections are really two separate events.

Has the Lord already alerted His disciples that an opportunity would arise whereby the righteous could escape the temptation of whether, or not, to accept the mark of the beast?

The disciples of Christ have been informed by the Lord that those who have kept the word of His patience (the commandments of God) would have the opportunity to escape the hour of temptation, which shall come upon all the world. *"Because thou hast kept the word of my patience, I also will keep thee from the hour of temptation, which shall come upon all the world, to try them that dwell upon the earth.[1] For as a snare shall it come on all them that dwell on the face of the whole earth.[2] Watch ye*

---

1. Rev. 3:10
2. Luke 21:35

therefore, and pray always, that ye may be accounted worthy to escape all these things that shall come to pass, and to stand before the Son of man."[3]

Just before the elect are resurrected, what will be the state of the world?

As a result of the rejection of the gospel of Jesus Christ, the world will be in the midst of experiencing the wrath of God. This wrath will encompass earthquakes, thunderings, lightnings, tempests, and the waves of the sea heaving beyond their bounds. *"And all things shall be in commotions; and surely, men's hearts shall fail them; for fear shall come upon all people."*[4] This is the tribulation or wrath that will complete the second woe and usher in the events associated with third woe and the sounding of the seventh trump.

Just before the first fruits are resurrected, what will be the state of the world?

It will be the time when Satan's great church called Babylon will have been bound in bundles, ready to be burned; it will be a time when the Lord shall alert His disciples that He will soon come as a thief in the night. Therefore, they are to remain faithful and maintain their watch so as not to miss the opportunity that will shortly arrive. And it will be a time when the armies of the world are being gathered to fight at Armageddon. *"And another angel shall sound his trump, saying: That great church, the mother of abominations, that made all nations drink of the wine of the wrath of her fornication, that persecuteth the saints of God, that shed their blood ... she is bound in bundles; her*

---

3. Luke 21:36
4. D&C 88:91

bands are made strong, no man can loose them; therefore, she is ready to be burned. And he shall sound his trump both long and loud, and all nations shall hear it."[5] *Behold, I come as a thief. Blessed is he that watcheth, and keepeth his garments, lest he walk naked, and they see his shame.*[6] *And he gathered them together into a place called in the Hebrew tongue Armagedden.*[7]

Where is the scripture reference that confirms the reality of a resurrection for the elect?

The Lord states that he will gather together the *remainder of His elect* from the four winds. These are they who are steadfast in obeying the commandments of God, and therefore they are rewarded by being kept from the hour of temptation, that is designed to try them that dwell upon the earth. *"And whoso treasureth up my word, shall not be deceived, for the Son of Man shall come, and he shall send his angels before him with the great sound of a trumpet, and they shall gather together the remainder of his elect from the four winds, from one end of heaven to the other."*[8]

Where is the scripture reference that confirms the reality of a resurrection for the first fruits?

"They are Christ's the *first fruits*," Joseph Smith records, as the Lord explains how this group will be resurrected and then descend with Him at His final coming. Thus, these are the remnant of righteous Saints who will overcome Satan and his minions by not taking the mark of the beast and enduring to the end. *"They are Christ's, the first fruits, they who shall descend*

---

5. D&C 88:94
6. Rev. 16:15
7. Rev. 16:16
8. JST Matt. 1:37

with him first, and they who are on the earth and in their graves, who are first caught up to meet him; and all this by the voice of the sounding of the trump of the angel of God."[9]

What strange heavenly event will precede the resurrection of the elect?

The sun will be darkened, moon bathed in blood, and the stars will appear to fall from the heavens and then shall the sign of the Son of Man appear in the heavens. *"And immediately after the tribulation of those days, the sun shall be darkened, and the moon shall not give her light, and the stars shall fall from heaven, and the powers of heaven shall be shaken.[10] And, as I said before, after the tribulation of those days, and the powers of the heavens shall be shaken, then shall appear the sign of the Son of Man in heaven, and then shall all the tribes of the earth mourn; and they shall see the Son of Man coming in the clouds of heaven, with power and great glory;"[11]*

What strange heavenly event will precede the resurrection of the first fruits?

There will be silence in heaven for the space of half and hour; and then the curtain of heaven will be unfolded and the face of the Lord shall be unveiled. *"And there shall be silence in heaven for the space of half an hour; and immediately after shall the curtain of heaven be unfolded, as a scroll is unfolded after it is rolled up, and the face of the Lord shall be unveiled;"[12]*

---

9. D&C 88:98
10. JST Matt. 1:33
11. JST Matt. 1:36
12. D&C 88:95

What trump will the angel sound to announce the resurrection of the elect?

The seventh angel will sound the seventh trump to announce that the mystery of God is finished; therefore, the dead in Christ shall be raised and the elect shall be changed from mortality to immortality, thus death is overcome as it is swallowed up in victory. *"But in the days of the voice of the seventh angel, when he shall begin to sound, the mystery of God should be finished, as he hath declared to his servants the prophets.[13] Behold, I shew you a mystery; We shall not all sleep, but we shall all be changed,[14] In a moment, in the twinkling of an eye, at the sound of the trump: for the trumpet shall sound, and the dead shall be raised incorruptible, and we shall be changed."[15] "And whoso treasureth up my word, shall not be deceived, for the Son of Man shall come, and he shall send his angels before him, with the great sound of a trumpet, and they shall gather together the remainder of his elect from the four winds, from one end of heaven to the other."[16]*

What trump will the angel sound to announce the resurrection of the first fruits?

Another angel shall sound his trump (which is the first trump), long and loud, and they who are alive shall be quickened, then they who have slept in their graves shall come forth to meet the Lord in the pillar of heaven. These are the first fruits who shall descend with the Lord during His Second Coming. *"And another angel shall sound his trump ... And he shall sound his trump both long and loud, and all nations shall hear it.[17] And they who have slept in their graves shall come forth, for their*

---

13. Rev. 10:7
14. 1 Cor. 15:51
15. JST 1 Cor. 15:52

16. JST Matt. 1:37
17. D&C 88:94

graves shall be opened; and they also shall be caught up to meet him in the midst of the pillar of heaven—[18] *They are Christ's, the first fruits, they who shall descend with him first, and they who are on the earth and in their graves, who are first caught up to meet him; and all this by the voice of the sounding of the trump of the angel of God.*[19]

Following this resurrection, another angel shall sound, which is the second trump: *And after this another angel shall sound, which is the second trump; and then cometh the redemption of those who are Christ's at his coming; who have received their part in that prison which is prepared for them, that they might receive the gospel, and be judged according to men in the flesh.*[20]

How, and in what order, will the resurrection of the elect take place?

The Lord shall descend from heaven and the dead in Christ shall rise first then those who are alive and remain shall be caught up to meet the Lord in the air. *"For the Lord himself shall descend from heaven with a shout, with the voice of the archangel, and with the trump of God: and the dead in Christ shall rise first:*[21] *Then they who are alive shall be caught up together into the clouds with them who remain, to meet the Lord in the air: and so shall we be ever with the Lord."*[22]

How, and in what order, will the resurrection of the first fruits take place?

The Saints, who are alive, shall be resurrected and caught up to meet the Lord in the air. Then the dead shall come forth to meet the Lord in the midst of the pillar of heaven. *"And the*

---

18. D&C 88:97
19. D&C 88:98
20. D&C 88:99

21. 1 Thes. 4:16
22. JST 1 Thes. 4:17

saints that are upon the earth, who are alive, shall be quickened and be caught up to meet him.[23] *And they who have slept in their graves shall come forth, for their graves shall be opened; and they also shall be caught up to meet him in the midst of the pillar of heaven—*"[24] Note, that the order in which the first fruits will come forth will be reversed from the previous resurrection. During the resurrection of the elect, the dead in Christ were the first to rise and then the living in Christ were taken. During resurrection of the first fruits, those who are alive will rise first, and then those who are dead will be taken.

Between the resurrection of the elect and the resurrection of the first fruits, what events will take place that are common to JST Matt, The Doctrine and Covenants 88 and Revelaton?

The following events are identified as occuring between the resurrection of the elect, and the resurrection of the first fruits.

The Church shall be taken into wilderness (places of refuge) where her children can be protected from the face of Satan's minions, the beast, false prophet, and ten kings. *"And to the woman were given two wings of a great eagle, that she might fly into the wilderness, into her place, where she is nourished for a time, and times, and half a time, from the face of the serpent."*[25]

Those left behind (if able) must flee to the cities of refuge to obtain protection from the false prophet and her efforts to force all to take the mark of the beast. *"And it shall come to pass among the wicked, that every man that will not take his sword against his neighbor must needs flee unto Zion for safety.*[26] *And there shall be gathered unto it out of every nation under heaven;*

---

23. D&C 88:96
24. D&C 88:97
25. Rev. 12:14
26. D&C 45:68

and it shall be the only people that shall not be at war one with another."[27]

The harvest of the wheat will take place. *And another angel came out of the temple, crying with a loud voice to him that sat on the cloud, Thrust in thy sickle, and reap: for the time is come for thee to reap; for the harvest of the earth is ripe. And he that sat on the cloud thrust in his sickle on the earth; and the earth was reaped.*[28]

And then the five vials of plagues shall be poured out as the harvest of the grapes begins: *And another angel came out from the altar, which had power over fire; and cried with a loud cry to him that had the sharp sickle, saying, Thrust in thy sharp sickle, and gather the clusters of the vine of the earth; for her grapes are fully ripe... And the angel thrust in his sickle into the earth, and gathered the vine of the earth, and cast it into the great winepress of the wrath of God.*[29]

At this point Babylon will be tied in bundles awaiting the destruction of the wicked. "And another angel shall sound his trump, saying: *That great church, the mother of abominations... she is ready to be burned. And he shall sound his trump both long and loud, and all nations shall hear it.*"[30]

Between the resurrection of the elect and the resurrection of the first fruits, how much time will pass?

Approximately forty-two months will pass away between the resurrection of the elect and the resurrection of the first fruits. We know this because this is how much time the beast, false prophet, and ten kings will be allocated to bring to pass the

---

27. D&C 45:69
28. Rev. 14:16
29. Rev. 14:15-19
30. D&C 88:94

harvest of the wheat and complete the abominations that will solidify their fate, which is, to be cast alive into a lake of fire burning with brimstone. *"And there was given unto him a mouth speaking great things and blasphemies; and power was given unto him to continue forty and two months."*[31] These forty-two months are also equal to one hour. We know this because this is how much time the ten kings will be allocated to receive power as kings with the beast. *"And the ten horns which thou sawest are ten kings, which have received no kingdom as yet; but receive power as kings one hour with the beast."*[32] Therefore, it follows that one hour equals forty-two months, or one half hour is twenty-one months.

Why is it important to know the difference between the resurrection of the elect and a resurrection of the first fruits?

It is important for four reasons: If there is a way to escape the temptation that shall come upon all the world, then every person living on the face of this earth should know about it so he, or she, can take the necessary steps to avoid this dilemma by embracing the true Church of Jesus Christ, and by doing those things that would qualify one to become an elect person.

Secondly, everyone should be aware of the trap the adversary will set (concerning the taking of the mark of the beast, in order to buy and sell) so they can avoid the snare that can prevent them from achieving eternal life.

Thirdly, all should know that if they miss the resurrection of the elect, they still have a chance of reaching the Celestial Kingdom, if they truly change their ways, reject all temptations to take on the mark of the beast, and dedicate the rest of their

31. Rev. 13:5
32. Rev. 17:12

lives to obeying the commandments of Jesus Christ. In other words, they must be willing to give all they possess, including their lives if necessary.

And finally, the righteous who miss the resurrection of the elect need to be aware that the Lord will provide cities of refuge where they and their families can find protection from the clutches of the adversary bent on bringing to pass their destruction.

In sum, these two resurrections (the resurrection of the elect and the resurrection of the first fruits) stand as bookends to one of the most important moments in time, which is: "the temptation that shall come upon all the world." *Because thou hast kept the word of my patience, I also will keep thee from the hour of temptation, which shall come upon all the world, to try them that dwell upon the earth.*[33] This is the moment when the big decision must now be made. *"Do I choose life by pledging allegiance to the beast and enjoy the privilege of buying and selling, or do I choose possible death by refusing to receive the mark?"*

For many, this decision shall be extremely excruciating. This moment will be eerily similar to what the early Christian Saints experienced, when a decision in favor of Christ meant certain death in the coliseums of Rome. For some, the thought of being able to maintain their worldly pleasure and possessions shall cause them to support the beast. Others, being more concerned with their relationship with God and His promise of eternal life and exaltation, will choose death.

Ironically, those who think they are choosing life by being able to buy and sell, shall lose their lives when the wrath of God is poured out upon the wicked, and their decision shall torment them for the rest of eternity. While those who choose death shall enjoy life with God in the eternal mansions of heaven.

---

33. Rev. 3:10

9 And the third angel followed them, saying with a loud voice, If any man worship the beast and his image, and receive his mark in his forehead, or in his hand,[34]

10 The same shall drink of the wine of the wrath of God, which is poured out without mixture into the cup of his indignation; and he shall be tormented with fire and brimstone in the presence of the holy angels, and in the presence of the Lamb.[35]

11 And the smoke of their torment ascendeth up for ever and ever: and they have no rest day nor night, who worship the beast and his image, and whosoever receiveth the mark of his name.[36]

---

34. Rev 14:9
35. Rev. 14:10
36. Rev. 14:11

32

Epilogue

For centuries the Lord has pleaded for us to come unto Him and He would show us the great things that the Father has laid up for us from the foundation of the world. However, because of wickedness, hardness of heart, and blindness of mind, these things have been hidden from us. In short, they have been concealed because of *"unbelief."*

If we could just rend that veil of *"unbelief,"* the Lord has said that *He would open the windows of heaven and pour out so many blessings that we would not have room to receive them.*[1]

What is the primary barrier that has thwarted us from attaining these blessings? For some, sin is the culprit. As an individual becomes entangled in the nets of indulgences thrown by the adversary, it is easy to think that all is lost. But the Savior has provided this comforting thought: *Though your sins be as scarlet, they shall be white as snow.*[2] Others are blinded from the truth because of unexplained trials and tribulation. In response, the Lord has said that *He was sent to heal the broken hearted, recover the sight to the blind, and set at liberty them that are bruised.*[3] Many do not believe, because they have been lulled into a false sense of well being by the comfort of surrounding

1. Mal. 3:10
2. Isa. 1:18
3. See Luke 4:18

circumstances and preconceived fictitious notions. *To these individuals the Lord cautions: Woe to the rich, for they have received their compensation, the full, for they shall hunger, the joyful, for they shall mourn, and the receiver of praise, for in like manner did their fathers applaud their false prophets.*[4]

At the present time a great war is being waged between the Church of Jesus Christ and the church of Satan. The Book of Revelation provides us with the knowledge that Christ shall win this battle, and that Satan will eventually be consigned to a place where he shall be tormented forever and ever. The decision we must make is whose side do we join. For those who want to unite with The Church of Jesus Christ of Latter-day Saints, these are the requirements:

Become teachable: *"Verily I say unto you, Except ye be converted, and become as little children, ye shall not enter into the kingdom of heaven. Whosoever therefore shall humble himself as this little child the same is greatest in the kingdom of heaven."*[5]

Have faith and repent: *"The time is fulfilled, and the kingdom of God is at hand: repent ye, and believe the gospel."*[6]

Be baptized: *"He that believeth and is baptized shall be saved; but he that believeth not shall be damned."*[7]

Endure to the end: *"He that endureth to the end shall be saved."*[8]

How can we know if all of this is true? This question is so important, that the Savior has told us to bypass less reliable sources of information and pray to God for the answer. For the Lord has said, *"If any of you lack wisdom, let him ask of God, that giveth to all men liberally, and upbraideth not; and it shall be given him. But let him ask in faith, nothing wavering. For he that wavereth is like a wave of the sea driven with the wind and tossed"*[9]

---

4. See Luke 6:24-26   7. Mark 16:16
5. Matt 18:3, 4   8. Matt. 10:22
6. Mark 1:15   9. James 1:5, 6